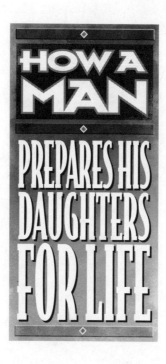

HOW A MAN
PREPARES HIS DAUGHTERS FOR LIFE

LIFESKILLS
FOR MEN

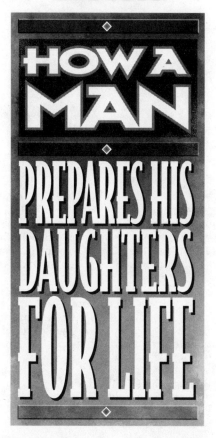

HOW A MAN

PREPARES HIS DAUGHTERS FOR LIFE

MICHAEL FARRIS

DAVID HAZARD, *General Editor*

BETHANY HOUSE PUBLISHERS
MINNEAPOLIS, MINNESOTA 55438

Published by Bethany House Publishers
A Ministry of Bethany Fellowship, Inc.
11300 Hampshire Avenue South
Minneapolis, Minnesota 55438

Printed in the United States of America.

Library of Congress Cataloging-in-Publication Data
Farris, Michael P., 1951–
    How a man prepares his daughters for life / Michael Farris.
        p. cm. — (Lifeskills for men)
    ISBN 1–55661–845–X
    1. Fathers—Religious life. 2. Fathers and daughters.
3. Christian life. I. Title. II. Series.
BV4846.F365   1996
248.8'421—dc20   96–10066
                                               CIP

To Christy, Jayme, Katie,

Jessica, Angie,

and little Emily.

Michael Farris is the proud father of a half dozen daughters and three sons. He is a constitutional lawyer and President and Founder of Home School Legal Defense Association, and with his wife, Vickie, leads marriage and family seminars. He and his family live in Virginia.

Contents

Acknowledgments

My friend David Hazard asked me to write this book because he knows my daughters. I am grateful to him for his trust in me and his skill in editing this book. My secretary, Sally, was a great help as always. Sally has a great dad who guided her well.

Introduction

I'll never forget that morning. The clean air of the Pacific Northwest just seemed to glisten a brilliant blue. It was a perfect Saturday in late June. In Spokane, Washington, where we lived, some men would go fishing, some would mow their lawn, and some would take advantage of the day for golf.

I doubt that many of the other men living in Spokane at the time have a clear recollection of June 28, 1975. But I do. It was the day I held my firstborn child—my daughter—in my arms for the first time.

I got to hold Christy even before my wife did. While the doctor and nurses took care of Vickie, I walked around the birthing room with a tiny bundle in a warm white blanket. Those unfocused eyes seemed to stare up into mine.

My life would never be the same.

Within a day or two, I made all kinds of resolutions to change, to improve myself, to be a better man. After all, I was now the proud father of a daughter. *A daughter!* I got a haircut. I promised Vickie I would have better manners around the house. And I would . . . and I would . . . and I *would. . . .*

Since that morning and all those promises, twenty years have come and gone swiftly. Christy is now grown and in college. And Christy has five younger sisters, not to mention three little brothers, so far. Our first five were girls, then a boy, then a girl, then two more boys.

Christy is twenty. Jayme is eighteen. Katie is fifteen. Jessica is eleven. Angie is nine. And Emily's almost six. Six daughters. More than most fathers.

I've had lots of practice with daughters. And with the Lord's help, and a fantastic wife, we have seen considerable success with our girls. The two that are essentially grown are attractive, smart, morally upright, and spiritually vibrant. And the younger ones seem to be following the same path. If we couldn't demonstrate a certain measure of success with our girls, I shouldn't attempt to write this book. But I'd never claim that I have been a perfect father to my daughters. Far from it. I have perhaps as many lessons to share from my mistakes as from my successes. Thankfully, I've also had the benefit of observing and learning from many spiritual men over the years, and their example has helped me through the rough spots and taught me right goals to shoot for as a father. I'm thankful for the godly men in my life.

There is an extraordinary pleasure in being the father of a daughter—a pleasure you no doubt share, or you probably wouldn't be reading this book.

My goal is to share some things I've learned so that you can be better equipped to be a dad. On the day *your* daughter was born, I'm sure your chest swelled with pride, too. You wanted to be a good dad—a *great* dad. And the desire to be a better father to that little girl still burns in your heart.

Let's fan those flames together.

Stumbling ... or Building? What Kind of Block Are You?

A chip off the old block. The very words connote a pride in their children that dads just can't hide.

Visit any youth sports game anywhere in America—or a dance recital, or school concert—and you will observe fatherly pride in full bloom. For a number of years I've coached girls' softball teams, and each has included at least one of my daughters. There have been some moments of real pride watching them play . . . like Katie's crucial hit in the softball semifinals one year against a lightning-fast pitcher. We won 1–0. And there was Angie's consistent fielding ability in a team of seven- and eight-year-olds that made her one of the genuine stars for the whole year. And Christy's pitching and Jessica's batting . . . and Katie's grand-slam home run that got her Christian high school team into the state playoffs. In a totally different venue, there was Jayme's starring role in "The Nutcracker" ballet. . . . I could go on.

I have seen dozens of other fathers exhibit this same kind of pride in their daughters—sometimes appropriately, sometimes excessively, and sometimes obnoxiously. But I steadfastly believe that fatherly pride is a good trait overall—and it is *very* natural.

Pride is a tricky word. Used in one sense, it describes a self-centered characteristic that lies at the root of the vast majority of evil deeds. But there is another characteristic—a positive quality of simple *admiration* and *joy*—that the word "pride" also describes. "Pride in workmanship" means doing a good job, producing quality. "Pride in our nation" leads men to fight and die for our country and its ideals. And "pride in our family" describes a man who sacrifices his own desires and interests to do what is best for his family.

This natural, God-instilled pride in our families has been on the wane in our nation. Men have been "looking out for number one" at rates that are truly alarming. Only 61.7 percent of children today live with their biological fathers.[1] In 1960, at a time when most of today's fathers were children, 82.4 percent of America's children lived with their own dad.[2]

This statistic measures primarily one thing—an increase in self-centeredness. *Me-first-ness.* Men and women today are much less willing than prior generations to exercise the kind of parental responsibility that should be the birthright of every child. The societal consequences of such widespread selfishness are the stuff of crime statistics, poverty reports, and the rapid decline of our culture.

But this book is not aimed at such fathers—the ones who have taken off. It is aimed at the men who have shouldered the responsibility, who have stayed home, who are trying to be faithful. And it is specifically aimed at men who have the special privilege of being the father of one or more daughters.

Those of us who have stayed with our families, or who have taken over as stepfathers, may have a false sense of accomplishment when we look at the world around us. We see so much flagrant irresponsibility, we can legitimately say, "If

I grade myself on a curve compared to *those* fathers, I'm doing pretty well." In one sense, hanging in there for the long haul, providing, going to all those games and recitals, is a very good thing.

Yet, we need to realize that God doesn't measure success in fatherhood based on the world's standards. Our daughters are so inherently precious in His sight that our effectiveness as dads will be proved by the unwavering plumb line of their lives—and certainly not in comparison with some deadbeat dad.

God has called us to raise our daughters "in the nurture and admonition of the Lord" as Paul told us (Ephesians 6:4, KJV). And if we heed Solomon's counsel to hold to God's standard of nurture and discipline, then our daughters will "give us peace" and "bring delight to our souls" (Proverbs 29:17).

Pride in our families and love of our daughters motivate us to be the best father we can possibly be. We shouldn't accept "good enough" or "second best."

In fact, fatherly pride can be life-changing. One young woman I know, Yee Seul, tells a story of her family when they lived in the country of her birth—Korea:

> We used to be really, really poor—destitute. My dad became desperate to the point of suicide. He was going to kill himself. He then saw me lying in the crib. He thought of my mother remarrying and what my life would be like growing up with a stepfather. In Korea, like in *Cinderella*, stepparents are mean to their step-children. Because of me, he decided to stick it through. After my sister was born, we came to America. Since then, my parents have been very blessed financially.
>
> My father is not yet a Christian. But his natural, God-given love for me allowed me to grow up in a home where I was taught good morality and sound respon-

sibility. Even more importantly, I came to know Christ as my Savior as a direct result of coming with my family to America. My father's love and protection for me changed both his life and mine.

Your role in your daughter's life will have profound, life-long effects on her. You will shape—for good or for ill—her ideas about a husband. And even more sobering is the thought that your actions as an earthly father will dramatically influence your daughter's view of her heavenly Father.

None of us will ever be perfect. Nonetheless, we have no excuse to be satisfied with mediocrity. The sad truth is that it is not only the children of absentee fathers that are at risk. Tens of millions of daughters have fathers at home who are often a stumbling block to their daughter's healthy growth and development.

Consider the following five examples of "stumbling block" fathers. Most of us have at least some of these characteristics.

Mr. Success

The saddest story in all Scripture, in my opinion, is the tale of Jepthah and his daughter recorded in Judges 11. It's got a lot to say to us as men and fathers about how far we'll go to prove we're right, and successful, and on top.

Jepthah was a man from the wrong side of the tracks who was seeking success. His father was Gilead, a leader of Israel, but his mother was a prostitute. Gilead also had a number of legitimate sons with his legal wife. When the sons grew up, they denied Jepthah any share in his father's estate.

I can understand why a man like Jepthah would have a greater desire to succeed than most men. He apparently had talents and leadership qualities. And through no fault of his own he was forced away from family, home, and an opportunity to serve and lead. Jepthah's opportunity to prove himself came years later when the Ammonites made war on Israel. His estranged brothers came to him and asked him to lead the army. It was a very high responsibility and, for Jepthah, a tremendous opportunity for the one big success he needed. He'd be on top at last!

Now Jepthah was no rank opportunist, no yuppy career climber. He had a healthy understanding of God's role in battles. Scripture records numerous statements which clearly indicate that Jepthah understood the battle belonged to the Lord. He was God's man. Today you'd see him in church . . . whenever he wasn't closing a business deal.

So far, so good. But then Jepthah did something extraordinarily foolish. Jepthah told the Lord, "If you give the Ammonites into my hands, whatever comes out of the door of my house to meet me when I return in triumph from the Ammonites will be the LORD's, and I will sacrifice it as a burnt offering" (Judges 11:30–31).

This wild vow was doomed to produce tremendous sorrow. What did Jepthah expect to come out of the front door of his house and greet him? How many times had he come home from work in the past, and out the front door came an ox or a lamb?

Of course Jepthah was deeply grieved when it was his one and only daughter who came running out the door to greet him. But we should not think that Jepthah made an innocent vow or that he merely suffered a terrible twist of fate. He probably expected a servant to come out and greet him. Maybe he was hoping it would be one of his brothers.

Jepthah did not intentionally turn his back on his daughter. He genuinely loved his little girl. He wanted to be a good dad. *He simply wanted success more.* And so he was thoughtless and made a rash vow.

We can be certain that God was not pleased with Jepthah's vow. Nor can we expect that God was honored in the fact that Jepthah kept it. When his daughter came out to greet him, he should have renounced his foolish words. It seems that pride prevented him. If he would have done so, he'd have had an opportunity to teach Israel that God does not give success on the strength of our verbal promises or our efforts. Our job, Jepthah could have said, is simply to be faithful to Him.

But in the final analysis, Jepthah's pride and drive to be respected were more important than the life of his daughter.

Modern fathers do not make vows involving altars and sacrificial killings. But we often set high achievement goals and promise to take time for our families later, with somewhat the same effect as sacrificing our daughters.

Like Jepthah, a Mr. Success kind of dad genuinely loves his daughter. He wants to do the right thing. But Mr. Success seems to make a lot of rash vows.

- "Yes, I'll take that temporary job away from home. It's only for a year."
- "She's little now. It doesn't matter if I spend a lot of time at my job. I'll be able to do more fun things with her when she's older. . . ."
- "I'm going to devote a lot of extra time to my career . . . just until I'm making $85,000 a year. Then I'll be able to focus on my girls."
- "Sure, I'll organize the church volleyball league. It won't take that much extra time away from the family."

Do we really think through the implications of our vows—or to use the more modern term, our *commitments*? When we're asked to take on an additional project at work that will involve especially long hours for months, does the promise of success, position, money, respect, or achievement snag us like a fishhook in the jaw?

Or maybe you simply don't know how to balance out the good and well-meaning commitments you make.

Your church may have yet another program—a very important program that really seems critical for evangelism, missions, or Christian education, or the building program. No reasonable Christian can question the value of success in such endeavors. But when we make the vow to take on "one more task," are we really thinking carefully about the impact of this vow upon our daughters?

You may not be sacrificing the literal life of your daughter by saying yes to too many good projects. But this kind of foolish overcommitment undoubtedly kills your relationship with your daughter on the altar of success, achievement . . . even so-called "service to God."

It doesn't matter whether your goals for success are financial or spiritual. Rash vows to take on good tasks will be just as devastating to your daughter as your inviolable vow to become CEO.

"Short-range plans" that we use to justify ignoring our daughters "for just a little while" are the plans of fools. Such plans are described in Luke 14:28–29 (Jesus is talking):

> "Suppose one of you wants to build a tower. Will he not first sit down and estimate the cost to see if he has enough money to complete it? For if he lays the foundation and is not able to finish it, everyone who sees it will ridicule him, saying, 'This fellow began to build and was not able to finish.' "

For most men, the ten years they estimate it will take to build the business becomes fifteen, then twenty, then twenty-five—and their children are gone. But let's assume, for the sake of discussion, that you can really pull it off— that you really are able to work hard for ten years and then spend a lot more time with your daughter after that. Have you counted the costs of this plan on what you are supposed to be building in your daughter's life and character? Thousands of men have attempted this kind of ten-year-plan and have found that at the end of the period they have lost their daughters.

What vows have you made about your own success? Have you thought very carefully about the impact of your vows on the life of your children?

I was recently confronted with a very important decision in my own life. In 1993, I ran for lieutenant governor of Virginia and lost by a narrow margin to the incumbent. As a result of that race, and some other factors, I had a very good opportunity to run for the United States Senate, and saw some indicators I could win my party's nomination. Of the fifty-five top leaders in the Virginia GOP, fifty said yes, they would support me.

One person whose advice I sought was Paul Trible. He is a strong Christian from Virginia who retired from politics at the age of forty-one after serving twelve years in Congress—six years in the Senate, six more in the House.

My two-fold purpose for the visit was to ask his advice about the personal sacrifices necessary to serve in the Senate and, once he calmed my doubts, I wanted to ask him to be the chairman of my campaign committee.

His advice about personal sacrifices was not calming at all. He told me that in his opinion it is impossible to be a good senator and a good father to young children at the same time. His advice was compelling. But even more convincing was a story he told me about his son.

His son was nine years old when Paul Trible left the Senate. Shortly after leaving, the boy was asked what it was like to be the son of a senator. Paul's son answered, "For nine years when we lived in Washington I never saw my dad, then he left the Senate and we moved. It's so much better now."

I walked into that meeting to ask a man to be the chairman of my campaign. Suddenly, I had to make a choice.

I walked out a non-candidate. I was not willing to sacrifice my children on the altar of success—no matter how important the mission, no matter how unique the opportunity.

There is nothing wrong with success in and of itself. But to obtain it at a time or in a manner that requires the sacrifice of the lifeblood of our relationships with our daughters is far too dear a price to pay.

Time is a great unit of measurement you can use to determine whether you love success more than you love your daughters. How much time are you personally spending to see that she succeeds in growing up into a healthy woman of character?

Father Knows Best

Some men believe it is a sign of weakness to ever admit to his children that he has made a mistake. Somehow this kind of dad believes that admitting error undermines his authority. Rule number one for such a dad is: "Dad is always right." Rule number two is: "If Dad is wrong, see rule number one."

The Father Knows Best kind of dad becomes a stumbling block to his daughter when he insists on always being right. It's always "my way or the highway" with this guy. He only "accepts" his daughter when her performance, looks, or choices please him.

I am very supportive of the concept of the authority of fathers in their home. Every one of us needs to know how to live and work under authority. We fathers can achieve that best by learning how to rest under the direction of God's authority, which is above all others.

Dads need to command a certain level of respect. It's important to be right. And there are times when you have answered the question "why" once too often, and it is appropriate to simply say to your daughter, *"Because I'm the dad, that's why."*

But sometimes we are wrong—dead wrong. And if we

think that our daughters don't see through that, we're only kidding ourselves. They know. From a very early age your daughter will know when you have made the wrong decision, snapped to an inappropriate judgment, accused the wrong child of misbehavior, or chosen the wrong tactics to respond to childishness.

Such moments are among the most important times of interaction you will ever have with your daughter. If you ignore the situation, you will plant seeds of bitterness in her heart. If you openly deny that you were wrong and bluster loudly about the house, you are not only planting seeds of bitterness, you are fertilizing and watering those seeds as well. Or you may admit you're wrong but never do anything to change the foul temper that controls you.

A father who refuses to admit a mistake, or to work at changing poor, immature behavior, reaps a daughter who refuses to trust him. How will your daughter know that she can rely on your advice? If she has seen you repeatedly refuse to admit to or change obvious errors, she'll conclude, "My dad doesn't know right from wrong, up from down, or good from bad." Your reliability is actually enhanced when you are willing to admit to the evident fact that you have made a mistake.

Your soft, self-deprecating answers on such occasions will prevent you from becoming a tyrant, a fraud, or a mere caricature in your daughter's mind. *A strong man admits and corrects his mistakes.*

If you want your daughter to believe that her father really *does* know best, then show her that you also know best when it comes to evaluating and correcting your own behavior. Admit it when you've blown it. Let her see you take steps to correct your mistake. She'll learn to believe that maybe "my father really does know best—almost always."

Sugar Daddy

Paul writes in 1 Timothy 5:8, "If anyone does not provide for his relatives, and especially for his immediate family, he has denied the faith and is worse than an unbeliever." There can be no doubt of the importance of a father's duty to provide for the material needs of his family. To fail to do so is to deny the faith—an extraordinarily strong admonition.

However, if *all* we do as fathers is to provide for the material needs of our families, then we miss so many other areas of paternal responsibility and joy.

A Sugar Daddy is a father who thinks his main job with his daughter is to lavish gifts and opportunities on her. He will spare almost no expense to buy her toys, gifts, trinkets . . . and later clothes, CD players . . . and later, a car . . . or to buy her "the best education"—which he thinks can be purchased at "the right" school. Her affection is his reward. At times he may resent feeling like the World Bank. His wife, parents, and friends may even razz him or tell him he's spoiling his girl. But he likes the rush of her admiration and appreciation and somehow can't stop himself.

The Sugar Daddy doesn't only buy junk. Some men will blow the wad on the most expensive colleges. A home in the "best" neighborhood. Some will spend thousands more than is necessary on their daughter's wedding. Only the finest will do for his little princess.

Few men set out with a plan to become a Sugar Daddy. Oftentimes, lavishing "things" on a daughter is calculated to assuage a guilty conscience for having spent too many hours on the job. Sometimes—let's face it—we're building monuments to our egos. And more often than we would like to admit, giving a daughter a present is a substitute and a shield because of our emotional inability to give *ourselves* to our daughters. People routinely ridicule such men, "He gave his daughter everything money can buy, but she still rejected him."

A woman recently wrote me a letter about her Sugar Daddy, and the guy who became his replacement:

I'm not sure who left who, but my parents divorced when I was five years old, so my relationship with Dad was contained to two-hour segments each birthday and Christmas, although he lived just ten minutes away. Add to that the fact that he worked for—or should I say was owned—by the railroad. Countless times my little brother and I sat waiting for him to pick us up for the day, anxious and excited, only to be heartbroken by the phone call that inevitably came, saying that he wouldn't be coming because he had to go in to work.

To make up for all the disappointment, I reason now, he would take us to the toy store and give us the run of the place, telling us to pick out whatever we wanted. What a thrill this was for us as children. Yet even then we realized what an empty gesture it was. We were delighted to be able to have "whatever we wanted," but somehow it didn't fill up that hole in our lives that was left by the absence of our father.

Fortunately for us, we did have a father in our lives, day in and day out, in the form of our stepfather. Although he wasn't very expressive of his love for us, what mattered most was that he was there each day of our young lives. A gruff sort of man, his love was shown as he went off to work each day in order to provide for us. We lacked nothing, and there were those moments when his love came out in the things he did with us. Moments spent teaching us to throw a football, ride a motorcycle, appreciate the world around us, and just being there to share life's everyday experiences. And it meant more to us than any toy in any toy store in the world.

Another cost that a Sugar Daddy must count is the materialistic attitudes his behavior tends to breed in his children. They begin to realize that the really important things in life are financial in nature. They see you investing all your time in making money and conclude, "Money is the most important thing to Dad." And then they see the pleasure that material things bring to them and they say, "I like material things a lot, too."

God may call your daughter to the mission field. She may marry a pastor. She may marry a man who has a more secular vocation but who chooses to live a more modest lifestyle so he can spend more time with his family. In any of these scenarios, a daughter who, from a young age, has become addicted to materialism is going to struggle with a very different lifestyle as an adult than she had as a child in the home of a Sugar Daddy.

This is not merely a matter of adjusting to changes in financial standing. I believe that a girl raised in a wealthy home can adjust to whatever adult life circumstances she finds herself in if she has been raised with the proper attitudes about money and "things." The key is her father. If she sees that he really values his relationship with her, then she will place far greater value on her relationships than on material things.

Giving your daughter "things" may make the adjustments in the years ahead quite difficult. Giving *yourself* to your daughter will teach her the value of real love that can carry her through the best of times and the worst of times.

Father Figure

Father Figure describes a man who is, in fact, the father of a daughter in name only. He's a figurehead. His name is on his daughter's birth certificate and occasionally he'll sign her report card, but that's about it. He's an emotionally absentee father.

The Father Figure sits hour after hour in front of a television instead of reading a book to his daughter or finding some other way to connect with her. He will sit fascinated in front of a computer screen chatting "on-line" with strangers with weird fictitious screen names rather than talking to his daughter. He's in the home. But he's really not there. He may even think, *I'm an adult. She's a kid. We don't enjoy the same things. So I do* my *thing.*

Men who are champion "channel surfers" have to seriously question their commitment as a father. They live in video virtual reality—but are virtually nonexistent when it comes to their real-life daughter. You will not learn to be a good father from Donahue or the news or ESPN.

Real life doesn't flicker.

The All-Male Dad

The All-Male Dad might also have a son—a son he relates to very well, or at least a lot better than he does with his daughter. He may say to his wife, "Honey, you raise the girls. I'll raise the boys." Or, if he has no son, he's at least excused himself from "the world of women." The All-Male Dad may be a guy who suffers from misplaced *machismo.* He's a dad who doesn't know how to relate to his little girl because she is female. Perhaps he wanted her to be a boy and never got over the disappointment.

Very few men will totally ignore their daughters. But an unfortunate number have this female-avoidance problem to some degree. An All-Male Dad will prefer to go to his son's baseball game rather than his daughter's ballet recital when both are scheduled at the same time. Some will never go to the daughter's recital even when there is no conflict, saying, "I just don't like ballet." An All-Male Dad will take his son to the basketball game, the computer show, the sports shop, or the hardware store every Saturday, but will make a lot of irritable comments if he has to take his daughter shopping twice a year. An All-Male Dad is a man who would prefer to have sons but is "stuck" with daughters.

Vickie and I had five daughters before our first son was born. While all of us were clearly happy at having a boy, it was very important to our girls that they understood we were *not* having a sixth child just so we could try to have a boy. I never wanted to leave them with the impression that having "only girls" left our life incomplete in some way, or left me "unfulfilled" as a man.

Sometimes our doctrinal view of the role of women in the church invades our own family in an inappropriate and destructive way. Personally, I take a very traditional view about the role of women in churches. But I want to raise my daughters with the understanding that in Christ there is no male nor female, just as there is no slave nor free (see Galatians 3:28). I fully acknowledge and rejoice in the principle that God created men and women differently. But I never want my daughters to feel any difference in their earthly father's love and attention, as compared to that shown to their brothers. There is certainly no difference in their heavenly Father's love and attention. Why should there be in mine?

Lot, Abraham's wayward nephew, was probably an All-Male Dad—undoubtedly the worst example in Scripture. When the two angels came to Sodom (see Genesis 19) to rescue Lot and his family before God's judgment, a homosexual mob appeared at Lot's door and demanded that Lot turn over these two men.

What did Lot do? He offered his two virgin daughters to the mob of perverts!

I have no problem with Lot's desire to protect the angels from the mob. But his priority should have been to protect his daughters.

If Lot had sons I seriously doubt that he would have offered them to this crowd. The apparent hierarchy in Lot's mind was:

sons, then strangers . . . then daughters.

It is reasonable to suppose that Lot's daughters knew what their father had said to the crowd. And the effect on their self-esteem must have been devastating. It is also reasonable to suppose that this emotional damage to these girls played a major factor in explaining their subsequent behavior. Lot's daughters decided that the only way their father could have his name carried on was to get him drunk and commit incest with him. After twenty-some years of being third-class citizens in their father's eyes, it's hard to blame these girls for being so terribly confused about right and wrong.

There is a staggering cost to pay when a dad treats his daughter as a third-rate child. And many times the consequences have sexual connotations, much like the situation with Lot's daughters. Perhaps not incest. But a girl who feels rejected by her father is a prime target for a smooth-talking guy who offers her some sense of male love, his acceptance and approval, in exchange for something: a trip to the bedroom . . . a life as his household slave.

How many daughters who end up in backseats, hotel rooms, frat houses, or even abortion clinics got involved in sexual sin in the first place because they were hurting, emotionally starved girls . . . who simply needed their father's love?

Our daughters deserve *first-rate* love from us as fathers. They are God's precious gift. Don't create a stumbling block in their hearts that may lead to staggering consequences. Don't leave them trying to figure out what it will cost them to be loved by a man. Don't be an absent father. Instead, give them lots and lots of *love, attention*, and *time*.

The figure of Lot brings up the ugly subject of sexual abuse. Rather than lecture on this despicable act, I'm going to let you read a letter I received from a Christian woman.

When I was growing up I had a pretty good relationship with my parents. On the surface everything still seems that way to everyone else, but underneath, everything is not as it should be.

You see, when I was twelve, my father started sexually abusing me. This lasted for a period of about two years. I have forgiven my father for what he did, but the scars that were left behind haven't totally healed. My relationship with my father can never be the same way it was before I was twelve because I don't want to let him close to me for fear that I may be hurt again.

Since that horrible day when I was twelve, I have always wondered what it would be like to not be afraid of my own father, and I have also wondered how other people's father-daughter relationships were. I have been very envious of those around me who have great relationships with their fathers—because that is something I don't think I can ever have.

I desperately wanted to change what happened so that I could actually have friendships with guys without the fear that is always there in the back of my mind.

I have a hard time with my relationships with other people because of the abuse. Trust is something that comes very hard for me. I just wish that my father had been the one to show me how to have healthy relationships with people, instead of leaving me to try to figure it out on my own. I have worked past most questions, but I am not sure that all of them can be worked past.

If that letter doesn't tear your father's heart out, you are among the living dead.

Pushover Papa

Father Knows Best is far too arrogant, too self-righteous. A Pushover Papa is just the opposite. He lets his daughters get away with just about anything. She is the apple of his eye, his cute little girl, and she can do no wrong.

A Pushover Papa may discipline his son forcefully—perhaps too forcefully. But the little girl goes without any discipline whatsoever.

I am a firm believer in—dare I say it?—spanking. When the children are little I will spank either gender for deliberate disobedience of a rule that they have been taught.

I guess these days it is necessary to say that a spanking is done with either your hand or a small wooden object such as a spoon. Spankings are only administered in moderation and only to the bottom. (Sometimes a slap on the hand is necessary for a younger child.) No other kind of physical discipline is either appropriate or wise. You will find yourself facing child-abuse charges if you ever strike a child on the face or head.

By the time my daughters reach the age of twelve or thirteen all physical discipline is over. (I haven't had any sons reach this age yet.) When disobedience occurs at the older ages, grounding, loss of privileges, extra work—and I assure you with nine children we always have extra work—are the typical punishments.

Whenever Dad is home, he should be in charge of all discipline. I believe you should relieve your wife from this task and take the burden off of her. Especially if she is an at-home mom, she has most likely been at it all day and needs a break. More importantly, as the leader in your home, it is your responsibility to shoulder these kinds of (sometimes unpleasant) responsibilities. Remember, it is important for you to keep in mind that discipline is mainly for training, *secondly* for punishment.

If your wife is reluctant to have you handle the discipline, it's probably for one of the following reasons: either you're too harsh, or you're a pushover, or you aren't training your daughters with long-range, character-building goals in view. In that case, you've engaged in petty, punitive discipline.

A Pushover Papa loves his daughter in principle, but he hates her in practice. If you love your daughter you will discipline her. This principle is forthrightly stated in numerous passages of Scripture. Consider just one:

> And you have forgotten that word of encouragement that addresses you as sons: "My son, do not make light of the Lord's discipline, and do not lose heart when he rebukes you, because the Lord disciplines those he loves, and he punishes everyone he accepts as a son."
>
> Endure hardship as discipline; God is treating you as sons. For what son is not disciplined by his father? If you are not disciplined (and everyone undergoes discipline), then you are illegitimate children and not true sons. Moreover, we have all had human fathers who disciplined us and we respected them for it. How much more should we submit to the Father of our spirits and live!
>
> Our fathers disciplined us for a little while as they thought best; but God disciplines us for our good, that we may share in his holiness. No discipline seems pleasant at the time, but painful. Later on, however, it produces a harvest of righteousness and peace for those who have been trained by it. Therefore, strengthen your feeble arms and weak knees (Hebrews 12:5–12).

If you are too much of a pushover, then strengthen *your* feeble arms and weak knees and take the necessary steps to moderately, lovingly, and without anger discipline your daughter when she needs it.

———

What about you? What are you doing—or not doing—that

makes you a stumbling block in your daughter's pathway to healthy, godly womanhood?

You *can* become the kind of dad who sets a healthy foundation under his daughter's feet. One who, with the help of God, other men, and your wife, paves a level path for her to walk into maturity. The work is not that hard, but it does take diligence and a willingness to step out of our own leftover immaturities from boyhood.

How about it? Are you willing to grow and change yourself, and to give your daughter the best gifts she can ever receive— strength of character, depth of soul, emotional health—and a glimpse of what the heavenly Father is like?

You can pass on a heritage of health and spiritual maturity. Isn't that what you want?

Don't wait another second. Begin *today* . . . and you'll find a lifetime of reward. In fact, *two* lifetimes . . . or more.

For Thought and Discussion

1. Have you made any rash vows designed to produce success that take you away from your daughter too often? What does your daily schedule tell you about unspoken vows that may actually control your life?

2. When was the last time you admitted to your daughter that you were wrong about anything? When was the last time you admitted a mistake about something important? Are you only willing to admit error when the issues are *trivial*?

3. What do you think your attitude about money is teaching your daughter? Do your actions and words tell her that things are more important than people? More important than her?

4. Do you ever say or do anything that makes your daughter feel that you would rather have a son?

5. When your daughter needs discipline, do you find an excuse to leave the responsibility to your wife? How do you think that makes both of them feel?

Notes

1. David Blankenhorn, *Fatherless America* (Basic Books, 1995), p. 19.
2. Ibid.

Building Blocks of Love

How do we begin to build a strong foundation for our daughters? Let's look at some basic commitments that successful dads use with their daughters to build character and positive relationships.

Lovingkindness

Every positive aspect of a dad's relationship with his daughter could be classified as "love." The term *lovingkindness* is a bit more precise to convey the idea that our daughters need our tender, loving watchcare.

A daughter needs her father's gentleness. She needs his protective favor. She needs him to intercede on her behalf against all who would do her wrong. Dad, your girl needs your lovingkindness.

There are two tendencies in men that tend to diminish our capacity for showing lovingkindness. First, some men need to be macho. We seem to need to prove that we are unfailingly strong—and by that we mean tough, invincible, uncaring. We have somehow got it into our heads that strong is the opposite of gentle and kind. Let's get it straight. Strong is the opposite of *weak*—while mean or harsh or uncaring is the opposite of gentle and kind. There is nothing wrong with a father demonstrating strength in a whole host of contexts. But remember, your daughter needs to *see* your strength, she needs to *feel* your lovingkindness.

Our second tendency is to believe that girls and women have the same needs and desires as men and boys. In a certain sense this is true. A quick look at the husband-wife relationship sheds some light on the important differences.

A husband needs his wife's gentleness. And a wife certainly needs her husband's gentleness. But women place a much higher priority on receiving gentleness than men do. If you are giving your wife only that amount of gentleness that you think you need for yourself, you have a woefully needy wife. You need to dispense huge amounts of gentle lovingkindness to your wife—far more than you would ever ask for yourself.

The same is true of our daughters. At the foundation of building a proper relationship with your daughter, you must recognize that she is a woman in the making. And thus, you will have to realize that her emotional needs and priorities are going to be infinitely closer to those of your wife than to your own.

Sometimes, just "being there" on a reliable basis can communicate real lovingkindness to your daughter. A friend wrote me a letter describing her father's reliability in her life:

> I can never remember a time when my father, as busy as he was, was not there for me. One thing that stands out most in my mind is that he never missed a ball game that I played, be it home or away. And believe me, in our conference, some of our games were really away! I played field hockey in the fall, basketball in the

winter, and softball in the spring. My dad always came to every game, and his voice was the one I heard over the crowd cheering me on or telling me how to play better. It didn't matter if it was forty degrees outside and raining; he would be the only parent on the sidelines of a field hockey game. In a gym full of opposing fans three hours from our home, I remember hearing my dad encouraging me to block out when going for a rebound.

This may not seem like a great deal to many. But to a young girl on the brink of womanhood, unsure, insecure, and a lot of times confused, it was nice being able to look up into the stands and see my dad. Always there, always rooting me on, whether it be praise or correction. His actions were a reaffirmation that he was there not only to watch my games, but to cheer me on in life. I never felt he was too busy for me, even though he was a very busy man. He made time to take an interest in what was important to his little girl. I knew that if he was interested in what I enjoyed, then he must be interested in me as a person. What a great thing to know that your father is always there, always waiting in the stands to cheer you on.

Your lovingkindness can be exhibited to your daughter in what you say and how you say it. But as this story shows, it's also seen in *what* you do and *how* you do it.

But make no mistake—lovingkindness in what you say is also vital. Take a quick self-examination.

How about your *general attitude* toward your daughter?

- Do you give your daughter far more positive comments than negative comments?
- Are there many times in a week when you praise your daughter for her actions or attitudes without mentioning anything negative at all? Saying, "Great job on your history test" (and saying nothing sarcastic or negative about the spelling test).

- When you say something positive, is it immediately followed by something negative? "You were very helpful
with the dishes tonight, but why is your room so messy?"
- When you give your daughter praise, do you usually urge
her to "do even better next time"?

In short, do you have a problem with giving positive encouragement?

If you have fallen into the habit of only saying something
positive as a prelude to some type of correction, your daughter
will only remember the negatives and will believe that you are
insincere about your compliments. She will begin to dread
hearing you praise her because she will know that criticism is
about to follow.

I know a woman who graduated number two in her high-
school class of over a thousand. The strongest memories of her
father during those years was his constant urging to do even
better next time. Great results were never quite good enough.
A little more excellence was possible. Now, decades later in
adult life, her tendency is to doubt her own adequacy, even
though she is clearly a woman of outstanding accomplish-
ments. Her father's tainted praise created, or exaggerated, a
natural tendency toward habitual self-doubt.

- Do you say please and thank you to your daughter?
- How about your correction? Is it firm *and* loving?
- Is the tone of your voice usually kind? enraged? businesslike? (If you think businesslike and kind are the same
thing, ask your wife—she'll be glad to explain the difference to you.)
- Do you refrain from sarcasm toward your daughter? Sarcasm is correction plus contempt. Your daughter will often
merit correction. She will never merit your contempt.
- Do you correct your daughter in front of others?

Sometimes certain mild corrections are simply unavoidable in front of other members of your immediate family (when you are riding in the car, for example). But the vast majority of the time, any correction you undertake—and certainly any serious correction—should be done in private. The only observer should be your wife—or another child if both were involved in a mutual misdeed.

Showing *courtesy* is another means of communicating gentleness, and it will clearly show your daughter that your love for her is marked by kindness.

- Do you mind your manners around your daughter?
- Do you open doors for her?
- Do you excuse yourself when you know you should?
- Do you interrupt her all the time because you have something "more important" to say or a "more accurate" point of view?

Communicating love also means letting your daughter know she is accepted just the way she is. Just *because* she is.

- Do you tell your little girl all through her life that you love her?
- Do you buy her a small arrangement of flowers to go with the larger one you bought for your wife on Valentine's Day?
- Do you hug your daughter regularly? I am a firm believer in playing with your daughters. But if your daughter only feels your physical touch in play or in a slap-happy kind of way, she will miss something important. In this day when men are accused of sexual abuse when they make a wayward comment or look, there is a tendency—at least I feel it—to be so overcautious with our daughters that sometimes hugging stops around age twelve or thirteen. Obviously, you need to be discreet and show a proper reserve with older daughters. But a dad should still be able to hug his teenage daughter in a manner that is totally proper and yet fully communicates his love.

- Are you quick to go to your daughter's aid whenever she has a real need? When she is young, that may mean scooping her up out of the driveway when she has skinned her knee.

Last winter I got a taste of what going to a daughter's aid might mean when she is older.

Christy was away at college and was sick for several days and was just not getting better. She could neither sleep well nor get the right kind of food. (She had to walk several hundred yards in the outside wintry weather to get to the cafeteria.) In the Lord's sovereignty I had a court hearing a day or so later only forty-five miles away. I ordered her to go to the nearest hotel with room service, and I jumped on an airplane that evening to see that she was squared away.

Christy and I know that I won't always be able to fly in on a jet to physically help her every time she is sick. But I believe that this episode taught her that her dad's love and protection is a lifelong commitment. And I think she knows afresh that I will do whatever is within my power to do to shower her with practical acts of lovingkindness.

Laughter

I am a big fan of fun. I believe in play. Laughter ranks high on my list of desirable activities. One of the unique characteristics of childhood is the emphasis on play. And I believe that a dad needs to be fully able and willing to play with his daughter from the earliest ages.

Dads need to color, wrestle, give "horseyback" rides, play that ever popular sport "roll the ball," and even be willing to (at least occasionally) pay some attention to a favorite doll. A good game of tag needs to be a part of every father's routine with his daughter. By the time my girls had reached the age of seven or eight, they loved to join in with our family and neighbors to play "capture the flag"—especially when played after dark.

I am a believer in organized sports for girls. And I have successfully coached girls softball for many years. Dads and daughters have opportunities for real positive interactions in these situations if done with a proper balance of striving for excellence while valuing participation and fun above winning. But your play with your daughter should not be limited to coaching organized sports such as softball or soccer.

I have taught my daughters to play hopscotch, jacks, and marbles. (And I hereby challenge any dad in America to a game of jacks. I am really good.) We play board games. We play a very "sophisticated" game called "Maid Marian and Robin Hood." I am the monsterlike Sheriff of Nottingham, and I sweep up one of my daughters—the designated Maid Marian—in my arms and start to take her off to jail. The others shoot make-believe arrows at me until I fall over dead. Then they all have to tickle me till I come back to life, and I start over by grabbing up the next "Maid Marian" with a roar. In other words, it is just plain, silly fun.

If dads are always work, always discipline, always orders, always serious, I think our daughters miss something very important. They will have a hard time believing that love is sometimes very lighthearted.

Play with older daughters is sometimes a bit more challenging. Silliness is not cool. And no matter how godly your daughter is, she will still have some type of "coolness meter" firmly installed sometime around her thirteenth birthday. The key is fun and laughter. Games and silliness are simply mechanisms to achieve fun and laughter.

I place extraordinary value on times late at night when my wife and I are sitting with our daughters in the kitchen (usually someone is seated on the counter) and our conversation is light, fun, and filled with laughter.

We have achieved a high fun quotient with our older girls

going to plays, concerts, skiing, water sports, and similar outings. From time to time, we play various games at home. At
least some games of the wilder variety are mixed in and are
invariably popular.

My girls have had plenty of opportunities to see their father being serious. They have seen me arguing cases in court,
preaching in church, giving political speeches, and adminis-
tering discipline. If they only saw the serious side, I think they
would be warped. I personally can't stand people who are in-
sufferably earnest. I want my girls to face the difficulties of life
and to make important, serious contributions to our nation,
but I want it all balanced with a lighthearted spirit.

Teach your daughters to take their work and their callings
seriously—but not *themselves.* There are too many joyless
people who take themselves too seriously. Being open to fun,
especially silly fun, requires a certain degree of vulnerability
that many men (and women) struggle with. We can't worry
about our images or ideas of self-importance. Get down on the
floor and have fun with your little ones.

Let me give you a word of caution about joking and teasing.
I love to tell jokes, and I believe that self-deprecating humor
is extraordinarily powerful. But there is a great difference between poking fun at yourself and poking fun at others. Never
make your daughter the object of harsh or demeaning jokes.
Making fun of her hair, her body, her poor math or writing abilities is *forbidden.*

And if you dish out the teasing, be willing to take *more*
than you dish out.

If you make your daughter cry or get mad as a result of your
teasing, you have clearly gone over the line. Don't tell her to
stop being so sensitive. *Apologize.* A little "good-natured"
teasing goes a long way. If teasing your daughter is a major part
of your "fun-time activities" with her, I would urge you to
broaden your repertoire and find other sources for laughter.

Learning

In Deuteronomy 6:6–7, Moses told the fathers and mothers of Israel to teach their children God's commandments by "talk[ing] about them when you sit at home and when you walk along the road, when you lie down and when you get up." In other words, fathers are commanded to teach their children as they go through the course of their regular daily living.

Spiritual teaching and learning is without a doubt the highest priority for all dads. And we will deal with this topic in-depth in the next chapter.

But teaching your daughter involves a great many more areas than the subject matters we would strictly think of as "spiritual instruction." Dads have a special responsibility to teach their daughters how things in our society work. In fact, the technical definition of "socialization" is teaching a child the rules of society. You and your wife can teach your daughter the rules of society—that is, how things *should* work—or you can let your daughter learn the rules from her friends, companions, television, and schools.

Many fathers have decided to home school their children in order to have the time to effectively and properly socialize their children. Others train their children in aspects of character formation and social skills, even if their children are in a public school or a Christian school. Regardless of *where* your child attends school, every father has the responsibility to insure that his daughter learns character development and good socialization rather than the bad socialization that is so prevalent in the world about us.

You can help your daughter get along better in life by teaching her basic rules of etiquette. Knowing how to behave in polite society will help her. Your wife will probably need to be substantially involved in this area of instruction, but you can make a major impact that will help your daughter for the rest of her life. You can help her also by training her in how to properly respond to authority, particularly her responsibility to obey the law. A father is the key authority figure in a young girl's life. The way you interact with authority will be watched and imitated. Drive with your daughter the way you expect her to drive when she gets her driver's license.

Your daughter needs to know how institutions in our society work. You can help her by explaining basic political and commercial practices—such as local and state governments, the Federal government, how churches work, how food "just appears" in grocery stores, where clothes come from, how we get our cars. These are the sorts of lessons about life that I mostly learned from my father as we rode along in the car. He would constantly look for ways to teach me all kinds of things as we went about our business on an evening or a Saturday. Keep in mind that speaking well of those in leadership can encourage your daughter to catch a vision of what her life calling might be—opening a world of possibilities to her.

It is, of course, very important to pay attention to your daughter's academic instruction, no matter what form of academic education you choose. From the time your daughter is able to sit up you can give her an enormous headstart by simply reading to her. A daughter who is read to will learn to read well herself.

"Kim" grew up in the home of an alcoholic father—not exactly an ideal role model. Nonetheless, she credits her less-than-ideal father with much good in her life. She wrote to me:

> One thing I really appreciate about our relationship is that he introduced me to good books and encouraged me to read a lot. I especially remember a thick volume of Jack London he gave to me as a gift. He just left it on the kitchen table one morning with the inscription: "Thanks for being such a great daughter."
> He also encouraged me to become educated (I'm the only one of his three kids who went to college—he

would have liked for all of us to go) and to develop my talents. I wouldn't be where I am today if not for his gentle prodding.

I have read C. S. Lewis's *Chronicles of Narnia* many times to my children. First I read this series to my three oldest girls a couple of times. In recent years, my younger two girls (ages eleven and eight) have been listening to the series for their second time along with their younger brother. They love it, and I have learned a lot of great spiritual lessons as I have virtually committed the series to memory.

Biographies of great men and women are other good read-aloud books. I have read *Uncle Tom's Cabin,* which teaches both American history and compassion for all people. Another favorite is *Kidnapped* by Robert Louis Stevenson, which teaches persistence and loyalty. But our all-time favorite series of books to read aloud to our children when they are younger are about the monkey *Curious George*—these are *not* classical literature by any definition. They are so simple that, frankly, we have a great time making up new story lines to go with the pictures. And this exercise lets me believe I am a great comedian—little kids will laugh at almost anything.

As you are reading, take time to occasionally stop to explain vocabulary, which increases word skills in children tremendously. School books are so dumbed-down these days. (In my legal practice I was involved in a lawsuit against a major textbook publisher several years ago. They took out words like "antelope" and substituted "deer" because antelope was too hard to read. And this was for an *eighth*-grade textbook!)

You can encourage a lot of good dialogue with your daughter on the issues of character that great literature often illuminates. To me, cultural illiteracy and moral decline are different symptoms of the same disease. We can expect nothing except substandard results from a generation left to itself. However, when fathers invest substantial time to teach their daughters about life, society, and moral character, they know more and live on a higher plane, as well.

As you are teaching your daughter, you will have many opportunities to demonstrate patience and love. A friend of mine, Carla, tells a story of a father's patience when he was teaching her to drive.

> One memory that will always stand out was the time I drove the family car for the first time by myself. I was nervous but excited that I was finally able to go to the store by myself. I drove a few feet, and as I was going around a corner another car was approaching me. It did not seem like much room on the road and I panicked and pulled right. Unfortunately, the neighbor's car was to my right and I hit it, causing a nice dent in their door. I got out and went home crying. My father came to see the situation, went with me to the neighbor, and then we went home. He was not angry and was amazingly understanding. After I calmed down a bit, he told me we had to go right back out and he wanted me to drive around the neighborhood a few minutes while he was in the car with me. Of course, that was the last thing I wanted to do. He said he did not want me to be afraid to drive again because I had hit that car, and that the longer I waited to get back in the driver's seat, the harder it would be. Although I still did not like driving for quite a while, I was always thankful for my father's response. I thought of it later in times when I felt like giving up on something, or when I failed the first time at a new task. It helped me to realize that it is important to face our fears and not be overcome by them.

Her *dad* taught her that.

Listening

Typical men and typical women communicate for different purposes. Typical men communicate to transmit information.

Typical women communicate to further a relationship.

Obviously these are generalizations and, accordingly, are riddled with exceptions. But it is valuable for you to remember that your male-communication style is likely to be quite different from the style your daughter desires, practices, and expects.

Perhaps the most important listening skill a father can learn is what I call the "Deli Maneuver." Go to any good delicatessen. Order something—let's say a pound of roast beef. After the clerk has sliced, wrapped, weighed, and priced your roast beef, he or she will invariably say, "Is there anything else?" That deli survives and profits by making sure that you have had every opportunity to fully express every desire you may have for items in the store.

A daughter needs to be able to fully express herself before you start dispensing information to her. This is especially true of an older daughter. Listen fully. And learn to ask, "Is there anything else?"

It is hard to always be perfectly patient and listen to the very end of your daughter's willingness to chat—especially if you've got a "talker" and you're the silent type who prefers quiet. But we should try to be as much like Phil Donahue ("tell me why you feel that way") and as little like Jack Webb ("just the facts, ma'am") as possible.

A little girl (from age three or four, through ten or eleven) will typically come to you with a series of questions. By patiently answering each question, you are filling her desire to build a relationship by dispensing a variety of information. But if you give *only* the shortest answer possible, you will frustrate your daughter's unspoken and perhaps subconscious desire to use this conversation to build a relationship with you.

If you pay attention, you can begin to learn how to converse with your daughter in a relational manner. Listen for relational clues. If you hear your daughter talk about her feelings, respond in kind. Tell your daughter how you feel about things. She wants to know what is in your heart, not just what facts or data you happen to have in your brain.

Another very good friend of mine, Pat, put her thoughts in writing for me about her father, a pastor, and his lifelong practice of talking with and listening to her.

> My parents lived very busy lives with church activities and lesson/sermon preparation. Dinner was always rushed, and my parents were always busy doing something for the church. As an only child it was sometimes very lonely, except for the almost daily activities revolving around the church. I didn't see much of my mother between her job and the church. As a result, my relationship with my father was much stronger than with my mother.
>
> But for me, the saving aspect of this very chaotic life was our evening walk. Every evening my father wanted to go for a walk around the neighborhood just to unwind (a drive in the car if the weather was bad). What else was there to do but talk to each other? I learned so much from my father and he became my friend. The time together was the cement in our relationship that weathered the difficult years when peer influences were so strong on me. For most of my contemporaries, the only time they spent with their parents was in front of the TV. We spent vacations camping and hiking and talking.
>
> I only got about thirty minutes a day of undivided attention from my father, but that is probably 100 times more than most kids get. It made the difference in my life. To this day, when I go and visit my family, my dad and I go for a walk every evening. It's what I look forward to the most.

What a dividend this wise father has reaped! Thirty minutes a day of walking, talking, and listening has produced a lifetime of memories. And a deeply cemented foundation of love!

That's what we're all after.

For Thought and Discussion

1. In what ways do you converse with your daughter in a positive, supportive manner? In what ways are you critical? Are you critical more often than you need to be?
2. Are you a fun dad or a stick-in-the-mud? How can you loosen up just a bit to make sure that your life with your daughter includes some appropriate laughter?
3. What things could you teach your daughter as you drive to and from your next outing alone?
4. Are you willing to keep quiet and let your daughter really finish before you stop listening and start answering?

Solving the Mystery of Spiritual Leadership

"David" is a computer programmer who is called in to solve problems only when no one else can figure them out. He is one of the most knowledgeable men I know about the content and meaning of Scripture. But David has admitted to me, "I really don't know how to be a spiritual leader in my home."

Any dad who has attended church for longer than a few months has been told: "Take your children to church, pray with them regularly, and have family devotions." Most fathers accomplish only the "taking-them-to-church" goal on a regular basis. And when it comes to family devotions, most dads fall down on this duty not because of the lack of desire, but because they simply don't know what to do.

The "church-prayer-devotions" trilogy is admirable . . . as far as it goes. But perhaps the reason that so many of us have been mystified about *spiritual* leadership is because we have started with this list of activities as if this were the totality of our duties as spiritual leaders.

Let's analyze spiritual leadership from a completely different perspective. Rather than starting with a list of activities, let's ask, What is a spiritual leader supposed to accomplish? The answer is simple, and challenging: A spiritual leader leads his wife and children toward maturity in Christ Jesus.

If we want to lead our daughters toward maturity in Christ, then we have to do three fundamental things:

- set spiritual goals for our daughters;
- design training and activities that will help them reach these goals;
- periodically assess how our daughters are progressing toward the stated goals.

At first glance, this resembles the mechanics of leadership we utilize in our careers. When a person knows where they are headed and they chart a course to get there, normally they are more successful than a person who simply wanders about engaging in random activities and opportunities.

If we want a spiritually fuzzy result, then spiritually random activity will work nicely. But if we want precise spiritual results in our daughters, then we need to formulate precise spiritual goals and create activities and training designed to reach these goals.

Setting Spiritual Goals

No army general would ever try to train soldiers in the haphazard way many of us try to train our daughters to serve our Lord. An army has an organized plan and a training course of increasing rigor designed to produce soldiers capable of winning the battle. Our duty to train our children is no less important. It is equally necessary for us to develop goals and plans for the training of the spiritual warriors whom God has entrusted to us.

A few years ago I taught an adult Sunday school class where we considered the following question: *What spiritual goals do we want our children to achieve before they are grown and ready to leave home?* We came up with a long list. With some editing, we ended up with the following goals:

1. My child will be sure of his or her salvation.
2. My child will love and understand God's Word.
3. My child will know and willingly obey God's rules of right and wrong.
4. My child will know his or her individual spiritual gift(s) and call from God.
5. My child will be able to teach spiritual truths to others.
6. My child will be an effective witness.
7. My child will spend daily time with God.
8. My child will have a servant's heart.
9. My child will be self-disciplined.
10. My child will be in fellowship and under the authority of a local church.
11. My child will understand the power of prayer.
12. My child will be maturely walking with God.

These goals are of a general nature that most Bible-believing dads will want for their daughters. These are a good starting point in the goal-setting process. You may want to modify these initial twelve goals, or simply choose three as top priorities. You will certainly want to add other goals that are designed specifically for your church background, your family's priorities, and your daughter's individual talents, gifts, needs, and desires.

Spiritual goal-setting should be led by you as father, but your wife should be intimately involved if she is also a committed Christian. And as your daughter reaches the age of eleven or twelve, and certainly by the time she is in her teens, she should also be integrally involved in creating the personal list of spiritual goals you want to engender in her life.

The twelve goals listed here are essentially behavioral in nature—that is, you can look at your daughter's actions and make a fairly accurate determination of her progress. Many of the additional goals you design for your daughter should also be stated in objective, behavioral terms. However, there is an additional category of goals which you will want to develop. These goals could be called "character qualities." There are several sources of lists of character qualities that we should desire for our daughters. Consider the following list of character quality goals based on the fruit of the Spirit passage in Galatians 5:22–23:

1. A mature believer demonstrates love to God and others.
2. A mature believer experiences joy in the midst of life's sorrows.
3. A mature believer experiences peace in the midst of the turmoil of life.
4. A mature believer is patient with difficult people and in difficult circumstances.
5. A mature believer is kind to friends and foes alike.
6. A mature believer consistently demonstrates genuine goodness of heart in all of his or her actions.
7. A mature believer is faithful to God, his or her spouse, family, and to other believers.
8. A mature believer is gentle to those under his or her authority.
9. A mature believer exercises self-control when people or circumstances evoke an unrestrained response.

Both the statement of these goals and the assessment of your daughter's progress will be very subjective. You would have good reason to be upset if a public school assessed your daughter's progress on matters of subjective values. However, subjectivity is quite appropriate within the setting of the family. You are perfectly entitled to assess your daughter's attitudes.

You can find a number of character (and some behavioral) goals for your daughter in Proverbs 31's famous description of the godly woman. You should also consider the qualities for elders' and deacons' wives listed in 1 Timothy 3. Even if your church has a doctrinal position of male-only elders (as mine does), there is nothing in Scripture to suggest that it would be inappropriate for our daughters to strive for the character qualities that are mandated for elders and deacons. Good character is always appropriate for everyone.

Both of these lists contain very important goals, but there is something even more fundamental that we need to remember as we work with our daughters. Consider the question asked of Jesus in John 6:28–29:

> Then they asked him, "What must we do to do the works God requires?"
> Jesus answered, "The work of God is this: to believe in the one he has sent."

Our most important spiritual goal with our daughters is to ensure that they believe in God and His Son. They need to know that God is both our nurturer and our corrector. That is what Paul is saying in Ephesians 6:4 when he tells fathers to bring up their children in the nurture and admonition of the Lord.

A nurturing father feeds and encourages his children in growth. An admonishing father corrects his children when they stray from the way. As earthly fathers we need to do both, and we need to help our daughters understand that their heavenly Father wants to play both roles in their lives as well.

Your daughter needs to know that God loves her when she makes a mistake, when she is seriously hurt, and when she experiences loss or even unfairness. She needs to know God's love—His nurturing love—in all of life's difficult circumstances. She needs to believe that God's love is bigger than any problem.

And she needs to know that God, her Father, will certainly correct her when she sins. You can help her learn to confess her sin—taking that candy bar "for free." She needs to understand that her sin grieves both God and the convenience store. And she needs to make it right with both.

Psalm 9 says that those who know God's name will trust in Him. God's names speak of His character. God our Provider. God our Defender. God our Righteousness. Taking the time to teach your daughter the names and nature of God will help her trust in Him all the days of her life.

Designing Spiritual Activities and Training to Reach Your Goals

Personal preparation

Recently, I interviewed Jim Ryun, the former world champion miler and Olympic star, and his wife, Anne, on my radio program. They are fine, committed Christians who have raised an outstanding family. I asked both Jim and Anne to comment on the issue of balancing the demands of Jim's career with his duties as a father—particularly his duty of spiritual leadership. Jim gave a fine answer. But Anne's answer was truly memorable.

She said, "I don't worry about Jim's balancing of career and family because I know that the first thing every morning—no matter where he is in the world—Jim will be up early spending time in the Scripture. And his number one priority in his personal devotions is a diligent search for fresh spiritual food that he can bring to his family." I had never heard this concept expressed in this way before. It had a profound effect on me.

I have a serious responsibility to bring spiritual nourishment to my family. It is not unlike my responsibility to bring physical nourishment to my family. If I want to bring my family food, I have to go either to the store or the garden and look for things that will not only feed me but all of them as well. This is the way I need to approach the Word of God on a daily basis.

For eighteen months I served as the volunteer pastor of our church when it first started. No period of my life was so fruitful in terms of my own personal time in Scripture as when I was on a weekly deadline to feed a flock . . . on *top* of all my other duties. If you have ever taught Sunday school or led a Bible study, you know what I am talking about. The teacher almost always benefits more than anyone else who hears the lesson.

What Anne Ryun helped me understand is that I have a lifelong responsibility to bring spiritual nourishment to my family. I need to be in the Word every day to feed myself and to get food for my family.

The next step, after your personal preparation, is to plan how you will train your daughter. Doing things God's way is not natural for your daughter. She is no different in this regard than you. She is going to have to be trained if she is going to routinely respond in a spiritually mature manner to the situations, issues, and decisions she will face throughout her lifetime. Let's consider two examples of how to design and implement goals for the spiritual training of your daughter.

Teaching your daughter to become an effective witness for Christ

God's ways are not our ways. We can easily see how different our ways are from God's ways when we examine our natural tendencies toward living for, and speaking about, Him.

The normal thing for all of us is to want to be accepted by others. We want to be liked. We want to have people think well of us. It is not natural to explain to people that they are sinners, headed for hell, in need of a Savior. That kind of discussion is confrontational, no matter how carefully you present the Gospel or sugarcoat your initial conversation. You are, in fact, telling the person that because of their sin they deserve to go to hell and they are in deep trouble that lasts forever, unless they turn their life over to the care and guidance of God in Jesus Christ.

So many of us are reluctant to speak of our faith because it is so very confrontational and just the opposite of what we would like to tell people in order to get them to like us.

If you are going to be honest with your daughter, you are going to have to explain—at least at some point in time—that her responsibility of being a witness can run the risk of appearing to others as unfriendly. We all know in reality that the most loving thing we can do is to tell a lost person how to come to Christ for forgiveness of sins, but we recognize that it may not initially seem so friendly to the one receiving the message when we're pointing out their mistakes and failures.

Your daughter's natural tendency is going to be to avoid speaking up about her faith or moral convictions if it will make others avoid her. And that tendency is going to become more pronounced as she gets older, unless she is trained to overcome her natural tendencies and to act in accordance with her spiritual tendencies.

How do you accomplish this? How do you help your daughter reach this spiritual goal? Here is a sample plan for two months' worth of training and activities:

Week 1

Memorize four to six key verses that are essential for presenting the Gospel. Make sure your daughter understands the meaning of the verses and the reason that they have been chosen for this purpose. As you memorize together, emphasize that unless a lost person receives Christ they are going to spend the rest of eternity in torment. Begin to pray every week for her unsaved friends with whom she would like to share the Gospel.

Week 2

Teach your daughter an organized method of presenting the Gospel such as the Bridge-diagram taught in materials produced by the Navigators, the Four Spiritual Laws, or material from Evangelism Explosion.[1]

Week 3

Have your daughter present the Gospel to you or other members of the family to practice the method.

Week 4

Have your daughter write her personal testimony of her own salvation experience.

Week 5

Have your daughter give her testimony as an oral presentation to your family. If she can't talk in front of your family who love her and share this goal, there is no way she will have the courage to share her testimony in front of a person who may or may not be receptive.

Week 6

Take your daughter along as you go to share the Gospel with someone. Or as you lead a study group. Tell your pastor what you are doing and ask him if there are any recent visitors to the church who would be appropriate for you to visit to share the Gospel and to have your daughter observe.

Week 7

Encourage your daughter to share the Gospel with at least one of her friends this week.

Week 8

Discuss the results of last week's sharing and encourage your daughter to regularly share the Gospel with her unsaved friends and acquaintances.

The best way to turn this training exercise into a lifelong

habit is to regularly pray for unsaved friends as a family and to discuss your own experiences in sharing the Gospel.

You could engage in this kind of training on a one-on-one basis with your daughter. Or you may find it even better to use this as two months' worth of family devotions. Younger children may not be able to participate in each of the steps, but from about age four and up, all of your children can at least pray for unsaved people and learn to memorize Scripture. And they can certainly watch and listen as "big sister" shares her testimony and practices presenting the Gospel.

Teaching your daughter to spend time in God's Word daily

From the time our daughters were able to read, we strongly encouraged them to read the Bible every day. In fact, it was pretty much a family rule that they had to read the Word each day. But their follow-through was a lot like mine—I would do it most days, but sometimes I just wouldn't seem to get around to it. It's not wrong for a father to want better things for his children than he was able to accomplish—especially in the spiritual arena. I really wanted my girls to read the Word of God every single day.

I tried an experiment that I thought might work. On New Year's Eve, about seven or eight years ago, I told my older girls that if they would read the Bible every single day for the entire year I would pay them $100 each on New Year's Day the following year. If they missed a single day, it would cost them $25. Each additional missed day would cost them $10. I made sure they knew it wasn't a bribe . . . but that I was sure they'd come to develop good habits.

Two or three years later, I was prepared to pay my older girls their $100 . . . *yet again* . . . because they had once more met the goal. But my oldest daughter, Christy, said, "Dad, you don't have to pay me anymore. I can't imagine going through a whole day without spending time in God's Word."

Her comment told me I'd reached the goal I was seeking. I wanted to create a good habit that lasted a lifetime. And a couple hundred dollars is a small amount to invest to reap that kind of reward.

This past New Year's Day my second crop of $100 winners—Jessica, eleven, and Angie, eight—have both completed their first year under my renewed challenge. If a plan ain't broke, I'm not about to "fix" it.

Assessing your daughter's spiritual progress

People rarely do what you expect. More often they do what you *inspect.* You will not know whether your daughter is progressing in her development toward the spiritual goals that you have stated unless you periodically check in with her to see how she is doing.

I would strongly recommend a weekly meeting (or biweekly at most) where you sit down with your daughter and talk over the assignments, training, and activity that she has been undertaking under your direction. You should also give her a chance to talk about the spiritual development and nourishment she is getting from other sources in her life: church, Sunday school, youth group, and, especially, personal devotions.

Not all the spiritual issues that are important to your daughter will arise in the context of your training program. You need to be flexible and listen to see where new spiritual needs arise. Sometimes you just need to listen. Other times you will have an opportunity to teach. And other incidents will generate new ideas for training and instruction to reach spiritual goals.

But I am convinced that unless we as fathers have an organized time for meeting with our daughters and an organized program of training and development, we are not nearly as likely to be involved with our daughter's spiritual life as we should.

You could design a chart to give to your daughter to help keep both of you focused, one that looks something like this:

Instructions: *Fill in items 1–4 as you begin. Fill in items 5–6 as you review your progress.*

1. Spiritual goal I am working on this week:
2. My comments on my needs in this area:
3. Dad's comments on my needs in this area:
4. My assignment for the week:
5. How did I do on my assignment? What progress did I make in reaching my goal?
6. Dad's comments on my progress toward my goal:

For a number of years, I took one of my children out to breakfast on Saturday morning. If this time works for you and your daughter, it's an excellent time for reviewing the events of the week in general and her progress on her spiritual goals in particular.

There are going to be rich moments of spiritual value that occur quite spontaneously between you and your daughter. But they are much more likely to occur, and will occur more frequently, if you have disciplined yourself to be involved on an organized basis with your daughter's spiritual training and development.

The importance of prayer . . . to you and to her

My favorite prayer memory involved saying grace at a pizza parlor when Christy was about seven, Jayme five, and Katie two. Just as we were getting ready to pray out loud, awful heavy-metal rock music started blaring. As I blessed the pizza I said, "And God, please, help this jukebox to malfunction or something to get rid of this horrible song." I didn't have time to say *amen* before there was a loud scratch and the juke-box simply stopped working. And we ate without musical "entertainment" the whole time we were there. My girls were very impressed with the power of this answered prayer.

Prayer is one of the most important ways that your daughter will see that God is real in her life. She needs to see some "jukebox" kind of prayers answered—where she gets an immediate answer that demonstrates God's ultimate power.

She needs to see God work through persistent prayer, as well.

Our younger team of girls, Jessica, Angie, and Emily, have been praying every day for more than two years that a family in our church would be able to adopt a baby. Several opportunities appeared on the horizon, but they all fizzled. Still, they kept on praying. All three of them. Every day. Month after month. Over the course of their vigil, our girls learned that adoption was very expensive. Just a couple months ago, their prayers were answered. Our friends were to get an eighteen-month-old girl (they had especially wanted a girl) from a source that would cost them very little.

I was very, very happy for this family—they are close friends of mine. But I was also very happy for my girls. I was glad to see them learn through this that God's answers are never slow. They could look back on all the other opportunities for adoption that had fizzled and realize that they were not as good as the answer that eventually came. They learned persistence in praying. They learned that God is smarter than we are when it comes to formulating the answers to prayer.

You and your daughter need to develop your own "prayer stories"—illustrations that prove from your own experience that God really answers prayer. But it is not enough just to experience these answered prayers—prayer stories need to be told again and again to continually prove that God is alive and working in your own family. They should become part of the oral tradition and history of your family. You definitely have such stories—like the time Uncle Milton fell over the ice bucket and landed face-first on the Thanksgiving turkey.

Some families keep prayer journals. Prayer requests are recorded. Answers are also recorded when they come. The journals become written histories of the power of God in your family. These are histories that need to be read—and read aloud from time to time.

Every Day

You will not be surprised when I say that you should *pray for your daughter every single day*. Pray for immediate needs. Pray that she will develop into a woman after God's own heart. Pray that she will find the young man that is God's perfect choice for her. Pray for this young man that God would keep him pure and that he grow strong in the Lord. Pray these and many other things for your daughter in her presence. And pray for her when you are alone.

You love your daughter very much, but not nearly as much as her heavenly Father does. Talk to Him about your little girl each day. Seek His guidance in your direction of her life. Ask for her protection. Ask God to prove himself strong to her again and again. Be persistent. He *will* answer.

For Thought and Discussion

1. What one spiritual goal would you most like to see your daughter develop? What steps can you plan to help her reach this goal?
2. How will your personal time with God change if you ask Him to show you new insights that you can share with your daughter?
3. Do you pray for your daughter every day? What areas of her

life, growth, and development are of most concern to you right now?

Notes

1. Check with your local Christian bookstore for the availability of these materials.

Save Your Heart for Me

One of the popular songs of the mid–1960s was "Save Your Heart for Me." From the title, you'd expect a message of purity and fidelity in romance. Ironically, the song was performed by *Gary Lewis and the Playboys.* And the lyrics conveyed the message that a person will engage in a lot of romantic flings, but hopefully your heart will be "saved" for that one true love.

We have been giving young people a lot of mixed messages for a long time on the subjects of love, romance, sex, and marriage. Conservative Christians have, of course, preached a message of abstaining from sexual intercourse until marriage. But then we allow, and even encourage, our older children to engage in romantic relationships far ahead of the season of life when they are prepared for marriage. Let me suggest that we are being totally unfair to our daughters (and sons, too)—not to mention unrealistic about human nature and the state of our culture—if we believe that our children can easily engage in sex-free romance.

At the outset of this discussion, we men need to get over the notion that this is a subject your wife alone should handle with your daughter. There is no question that your wife will play a special, and perhaps more confidential, role with your daughter on this subject than you will. "Wendy," a friend, recently told me:

> One thing I always wished my father would talk to me about was guys, dating, and sex. He would never discuss it. My mother did a minimum, hoping my dad would pick up the slack. As a result I learned from friends—not the best, by far. I did not have any brothers, so having a dad who was not very communicative in many areas was hard.

Dad, why would you let your daughter learn about this critical area from passersby? It's your responsibility. You should start when she is young. And you need to stay involved for the long run.

Think ahead to your daughter's wedding. When she walks down that aisle, you undoubtedly want her to be physically pure. (And you certainly want the same thing from the young man she's about to marry.) But you really want more than that. You want your daughter to love her husband-to-be with a singular, undivided heart. And, again, you want him to love her in the same way. You want both of them to be able to say with complete integrity, "I will love you with all of my heart."

The reality these days is that many brides and grooms can only say, if they are honest, that they love each other with the pieces and shreds of their hearts that remain. Usually they have fallen in and out of "love" numerous times. And often there has been some degree of physical involvement in these past relationships. We readily recognize that serious *physical* involvement in the past leads to challenges that must be overcome in a marriage. What we need to learn to recognize is that past serious *emotional* involvement also has long-range consequences that can be like so much baggage in a marriage.

A few years ago, I went to my twenty-fifth high school reunion. There I saw a classmate who had been my girlfriend when I was in the third grade. Yes. Third Grade. I was eight. I realized when I first saw her again that there was a momentary *plunk* on my heart strings that said, "I once had a relationship with her." I had given away a piece of my heart to her before I had lost all my baby teeth!

There were a number of other "old girlfriends" at this same reunion. And when I honestly looked into my own heart, I realized that I had foolishly engaged in relationships, wondering which of these girls might be "the one," years and years before I could legitimately consider marriage.

When I was in high school I struggled with trying to avoid becoming too physical in relationships with girls. I believed that everything would be fine if I observed a proper line of physical purity. I now understand that I was missing a more fundamental point. I needed to be concentrating on *emotional purity*. Physical abstinence protects the body; emotional abstinence protects the heart.

Now Vickie and I realize we have raised our daughters in a radically different manner from the rest of the world—even much of the Christian world—in terms of dating, romance, sex, and marriage. From their youngest days, the single most important thing I wanted my daughters to know is this: *Romantic relationships are reserved for the season of life when both you and the young man are prepared to be married.*

Our oldest, Christy, was first asked out on a date when she was thirteen. The young man, from our church, was sixteen. She looked at him and, in effect, said, "I'm not ready to get married. Why would I want to go on a date?" Needless to say, he was floored.

Today, Christy is twenty, Jayme is eighteen, and Katie is fifteen. I think I have beautiful daughters. But none of them have ever dated, and they have no complaints. If anything, they are far more committed to our philosophy of saving their hearts for marriage than my wife and I are.

Christy is in her second year in college. When she went away (she told us later) she was still committed to our principles, but she had real doubts about how it would work in practice. In the spring of her freshman year, she called us one night and thanked us profusely for raising her to save her heart for marriage. She said it was "Kleenex season" in her dorm. Every night, some girl was being dumped by the boy she had fallen in love with back in the fall. Christy and her friends were called upon to bring some Kleenex and comfort the girl whose world had just fallen apart. After watching the despair that "casual" romance brought to these girls, Christy was even more glad that she had been taught to practice both emotional and physical abstinence.

Sure, the world can object, saying, "But dating is *normal*." It may be *usual*, but how can we say, in the face of so much turmoil and emotional preoccupation, that it's *normal*? Think about it, dads.

I challenge you to discuss this area carefully with your wife before making any radical or hard-line decisions. You will need to be one in heart and mind.

On the other hand, our three girls have gone out many, many times with young men *in groups*. And when I say in groups I do not mean a dozen young people paired up in twos. I mean a group of young men and a group of young women who go out for a social event, with no pairing off whatsoever.

One of the young men who is in their circle of friends told me that he really likes the relief of being in a group of young people who are not under any pressure to pair off. He wants to be a lawyer, and he is about three years away from achieving that goal. He knows that until he can provide for a family, he really is not in a position to get married. So until then, he is very happy to have a number of young ladies as friends with no pressure to pick "the one."

This kind of practice allows our daughters to meet young men, and watch and observe. They are forming opinions about traits they like and traits they don't like, without getting crushed and rejected and used in the process. They have the opportunity to see characteristics that help them evaluate what kind of husband they want in a few years. But it is all done in a context where both emotional and physical purity are valued and maximized.

We call this philosophy *"courtship"* as opposed to dating. There really aren't a lot of rules for courtship. We have taught our girls basically just three rules:

1. I will not engage in a romantic relationship until both the young man and I are in the season of life when we are ready to be married.

2. I will investigate a young man only if he appears to meet the spiritual and character qualifications my parents and I have agreed to for a husband.

3. I will investigate a young man only if I find him to be personally interesting and attractive.

Most people use only the "interesting and attractive" criteria. And I want my daughters to know that this is perfectly appropriate to consider. Some people we have heard teach on this subject have asserted that physical attraction is unspiritual. I say: Go read the *Song of Solomon*. It's easy to figure out that God intended physical attraction and sexual passion to be an important part of a romantic relationship.

We have also taught our daughters that a young man is not ready for marriage until he is ready to provide for a family, maintain a home, and be a father. Scripture teaches young men, "Finish your outdoor work and get your fields ready; after that, build your house" (Proverbs 24:27). And, "If anyone does not provide for his relatives, and especially for his immediate family, he has denied the faith and is worse than an unbeliever" (1 Timothy 5:8).

A young woman is ready for marriage when she is prepared to be a mother, take care of a home, and to teach her children.

To do these things we have ensured that our daughters are taught childcare skills, homemaking skills, and academic skills. We want our daughters to have career preparation as well, but for a reason that's different from many other people. (More about this in Chapter 7.)

We began to teach our daughters this radically different philosophy from a very young age. We do not tease about crushes, boyfriends, or girlfriends with our children. I remember being teased about this as a child. Not only was it embarrassing, but it left an impression on me that it was appropriate for me to be engaged in "puppy love."

A few years ago, I took my son Michael to buy a pair of shoes when he was about four. The shoe salesman asked Michael, "Who's your girlfriend, boy?" I replied, "Mommy's your girlfriend, right?" Michael was clueless.

The world around us thinks it's cute when a four-year-old has a "girlfriend." They are not quite as thrilled when a thirteen-year-old gets pregnant. But make no mistake about it. The reason most thirteen-year-olds get pregnant is that they have been engaging in boy-girl relationships for a number of years. Over time, emotional involvement leads to some physical involvement, which ultimately leads to sexual intercourse.

Dr. James Dobson, as well as others, has helped to popularize the concept of "purity rings." These rings signify a commitment to remain physically pure until marriage. We enthusiastically endorse this idea. We have given both Christy and Jayme nice rings with real stones (around $100) on their sixteenth birthdays. These rings symbolize that they are going to save themselves for their husbands.

But in our case it is a recommitment to emotional as well as physical purity. We have found, along with other parents who have tried the same approach, *it works*.

If you listen to Christian speaker and teacher Josh McDowell, you will become aware that Christian teenagers are engaging in just about the same level of sexual activity as the un-saved.

Consider the "typical" pregnant teenage Christian girl. She may have attended a Christian school or been home schooled. She certainly attended a good church. She was raised by fine parents. What happened?

In many, many cases she was allowed to date. Around thir-teen or fourteen she started dating a boy who eventually fa-thered her child.

Her parents allowed her to date under terms and condi-tions that they had practiced when they were growing up. They knew there would be temptations, but they had per-formed admirably and without sexual involvement. Or even if they didn't, they somehow expected their daughter to do so.

The sad reality is this: Our daughters live in a different world than we did. When we were growing up in the 1960s, some areas of secular society still endorsed the concept of sex-ual restraint in dating. That is no longer true. TV, movies, lit-erature, public school sex education courses, most teen-agers—and even some parents—say, "It's natural. Just be careful." In the past, a young girl may have fooled around a bit, but she would have felt guilty to consider sexual activity. But in today's culture what restraints are left? Even the fear of contracting AIDS is seldom a deterrent.

By way of contrast, Christy is just now on the preliminary steps of her first-ever romantic relationship. A young man who is nearing the end of his career preparation has come on the scene. I know him very well and have spent a great deal of time with him. He has spiritual character and a real poten-tial as a husband, father, and provider. My wife and I recently took him out for an evening—with our three older daughters. There has been absolutely no physical involvement between Christy and this young man—not even one kiss.

A father's involvement in helping to check out a potential suitor is particularly crucial. A father shouldn't make the *choice*—the daughter should. But his insights and counsel are critical. Our daughters are well trained to know that any initial inquiries from any young man are to be directed to me. And when such inquiries have come, our girls have usually said, "Don't you dare say yes. He's a creep."

The young man who is "circling the landing strip" in Christy's life spent eighteen hours a day, three or four days a week with me a couple years ago. He was a driver for my campaign for lieutenant governor of Virginia. Obviously I got to know him quite well, even though I had known him from church for a number of years prior to the campaign.

Not every dad can spend that amount of time with a young man. But I would recommend that you spend as much time as you possibly can with a potential suitor. Seeing him in a number of ordinary life situations will help give you insights that will provide you with a much more credible platform for counseling your daughter. Telling her, "I don't know what it is, there's just something about him I don't like," usually doesn't sit too well with a young woman. If you have to point out flaws in character, it is better to have specific examples and actual experience. Such gut-level impressions are often right. But sometimes they are wrong. Your daughter will give you credence if you have spent the time.

We live in a sex-crazed world. Our girls are fully aware of the facts of life and have been so for many years. Details were taught by their mother around age twelve. They are aware by implication that Vickie and I enjoy each other's physical company. They see us kiss. They see us hug. We never tell them that sex is bad. By our lives and our words we simply have told them that sex is great in marriage. It is a disastrous misuse of God's gift in any other context.

But frankly, this message has sunk in a whole lot more effectively because we have kept the physical and emotional parts of love and romance linked together. Women want emotion and sex to be linked. Men are more willing to divorce the two parts of love. Your daughter will readily accept the concept of keeping sex and love united in marriage.

Teach your daughter to save her heart for her husband and you will have little trouble convincing her to live a physically pure life in the midst of a thoroughly rotten world.

After all, didn't our Lord himself teach us that it was the heart that was the key to sexual purity? He gave the instruction. I can vouch that it really does work in these last days of the twentieth century.

After you have worked through your own evaluation of this subject, and have come to the standards that you would like to follow with your daughter, consider one further piece of very sensible advice that was modeled by a good friend of mine.

My friend's daughter was nine at the time of this incident. He and his wife believe in virtually the same philosophy of courtship that I have just described for you.

One day my friend David and his daughter were engaging in casual conversation about the kids in the neighborhood— most of them boys. As David expressed interest in the conversation, his daughter said that her "feelings were overflowing" for a certain boy about three years older than she. David says, "I could have taken this opportunity to preach on the necessity of the 'equal yoke' (since the boy was unsaved), moral virtue, or could have introduced the concept of courtship. Fortunately, I did not. Instead, I simply listened and acknowledged that those feelings are natural and normal, put there by God. By acceptance of her emotions, I have given the confidence and freedom to my daughter to reveal them to me.

"On another day, when the feelings were not so 'overflowing,' we talked about what to do with those feelings—also about flirting, moral excellence, and courtship."

A wise father knows *when* to teach . . . and when to simply listen to his daughter's heart. Listening and not preaching or "correcting" her viewpoint will gain you her trust.

Do you want to raise a daughter who becomes a woman of moral strength and excellence? Then free her from the pressure of needing to "pair off" while she is young.

Katie was on the phone the other night with a young man who was emotionally distraught with a crush on her. She explained to him that she wasn't ready for a relationship with anyone at this stage of her life, because at fifteen, she is nowhere near the season of life for marriage. He wasn't offended because he wasn't personally rejected. And he seemed to consider changing his own ideas after their talk.

A girl who is free to say no to all guys when she is too young won't be pressured into moral compromise because of emotional responses to "young love." Moral excellence is built on a foundation of emotional abstinence.

For Thought and Discussion

1. Did your early romantic relationships do anything good for the young lady who was the object of your affections? Honestly?
2. Would you suffer as many temptations toward other women if you had taught your heart the discipline of emotional abstinence while you were in your youth? How would this discipline help your daughter when she is grown?
3. What kind of activities can you help your daughter find so that she is exposed to young men in a group without feeling pressure to pair off?

5

Guiding Your Daughter Toward Positive Friendships

When I was a very young lawyer in Spokane, Washington, I was assigned to defend a case in which two professing Christians, "Steve" and "Lana," were getting a divorce. Lana was seeking a divorce because of the advice of her "friends." She and Steve, my client, got into an argument one evening and he grabbed her by the arm and squeezed. He left a bruise on her arm about the size of a quarter. He was ashamed of the action—as he should have been—and he apologized. But it was a far cry from the "battered-woman syndrome." Lana was told by her friends, however, that she was a victim of wife abuse and she should seek a divorce. Believe it or not, she did.

A few weeks later her friends advised Lana that she should start dating, even though Steve was actively seeking to reconcile the marriage. One night when Lana was out on a date, their two-year old son fell behind the bunk bed and died from strangulation.

Lana knew what God expected of her regarding forgiveness and reconciliation, but she listened to her friends instead. She paid a terrible price for the wrong advice from the wrong kind of friends.

As dads, we know that we need to be concerned about our daughters' friendships because we recognize that childhood and teenage friends—like adult friends—have a big effect on our daughters. But we need to realize that guiding our daughters toward positive friendships involves more than just getting them through the formative years. A girl who is taught to form good friendships when she is young—and who is taught how to counterbalance a friend's advice with both God's Word and other counsel—will more wisely manage her friendships as an adult.

I was driving through a neighborhood in our small town recently when I saw a woman I'll call "Bev," whose daughter is a friend of one of our girls. I stopped and we chatted since we hadn't seen each other in a while. "Cindy" and our daughter weren't spending as much time together as they had when they had played on a sports team together in the past.

After a couple minutes of chitchat Bev said, "I am really worried about Cindy. I think she's falling in with the wrong crowd. She's probably smoking. Maybe worse."

In the past few months when I had seen Cindy around town, she was hanging around with kids who appeared to give a good basis for her mother's anxiety.

Bev's confession presented me with a dilemma. How much involvement do I allow my daughter to have with Cindy? How can my daughter be a *good* influence on Cindy, without Cindy being a *bad* influence on her?

Friendships are not neutral. Interaction between two people usually results in some kind of movement—up or down—in values and behavior. Far more often than not, given the sinful nature of humankind, friendships drag at least one person in a negative direction. But isolation is not a healthy choice for anyone.

Dads, we have a real challenge if we desire to guide our daughters toward friendships that lift both parties up in a positive direction.

About twelve years ago, we lived in a neighborhood about twenty-five miles closer to Washington, D.C., than where we live today. The very day we moved into the neighborhood a number of girls descended upon our home to make friends with Christy, Jayme, and Katie, who were about eight, six, and three.

Virtually all of the girls in that neighborhood seemed to come from responsible, moral families. Many were active in churches, although none appeared to come from homes that shared our evangelical religious traditions. These new friends seemed to be perfectly acceptable in almost every way. Every way but one.

A number of these girls used God's name in vain—not in a string of swear words, just a flippant and inappropriate use of God's name every now and then.

I knew from my own negative experience in junior high and high school that children pick up bad language, and it sticks first in the brain and ultimately begins to come out of the mouth. I wanted to protect my relatively young daughters from picking up bad verbal habits from these friendships.

Vickie and I encouraged our daughters to simply tell their friends, "We don't use God's name in our house except when we are talking to Him, or are really talking about Him." They did—it was well received by their friends. In fact, the entire circle of friends seemed to enforce that standard on the whole neighborhood. Good friendships bloomed that we have always viewed as positive for all concerned. A polite stand was taken by our daughters which resulted in pulling their friends in a good direction.

A few years later, Jayme, our second daughter, was getting involved in a very close friendship with a girl she knew at ballet. This girl seemed nice enough, but she came from a home that was in great spiritual confusion at the time. One parent professed to being a born-again Christian, the other parent yoyoed back and forth between our church and a church that most evangelicals would consider far outside the limits of biblical Christianity. There was a general lack of stability in the home. All of this made me doubt whether I wanted Jayme to be spending a lot of time with this girl. A friendship was okay. A close friendship concerned me. An intimate friendship had me worried.

I had a lot of trust in Jayme's spiritual maturity—even though she was only twelve or so at the time. But no matter how mature she was, an influence is still an influence.

After some initially unworkable ideas to try to limit this friendship, I finally told Jayme that I would approve of a very close friendship only if she and her friend would have a regular Bible study together. I told her that this girl certainly needed such spiritual input. Also, I really didn't want Jayme to have such a close friendship without a spiritual dimension to it.

Jayme agreed with my plan, went to the Christian bookstore, bought an appropriate Bible study, and began a weekly study with her friend between ballet classes.

That was about six years ago. That girl is still one of Jayme's best friends. She is clearly a Christian. She has grown in spiritual maturity. And her family has made a remarkable turnaround for God. It would be an exaggeration to say that Jayme and the girl's friendship was the catalyst in that family's spiritual renewal. But I believe it helped. When the one parent dallied with the idea of returning to the "other" church, there was hesitation because they didn't want to disturb the friendship between Jayme and their daughter. Relationships are one of the strongest drawing cards in any church decision.

Another girl in our circle of friends went through a very rebellious period. She left home and lived with other relatives a couple hours from her home. She fell in with a group of friends she describes as "really into the party scene." The prevailing morality was "everything is okay." In her own words, "There were no limits, and I went with that." She admitted that she was the kind of person who gives in to peer pressure. In her case, peer pressure culminated in her giving birth out of wedlock.

When she came home to have the baby (and give it up for adoption), her parents did their best to involve her with a new circle of positive, mostly Christian friends. Now, partly because of her father's influence and planning, she feels that her more appropriate friends help to guide her "back on track" when she is tempted to veer off again. She says of her friends now, "They encourage me to do what's right but don't point their finger at me."

To a kid, parental encouragement to do right always seems to feel like there's some finger-pointing involved. A positive friend can reinforce the parents' standards in a way that is not nearly as threatening.

You can tell the stories just as well. We all know it is true. There are good friendships. And there are bad friendships.

Here are a few suggestions that we have found to be helpful in carrying out our responsibility as parents to guide our children toward positive friendships:

Friends of your daughter should not be strangers to you.

We have a saying at our house: "An informed dad is a happy dad." This usually applies to situations when our older daughters are going to get home later than previously thought. But it is even more applicable concerning friendships. You should have at least some knowledge of your daughter's significant friends.

This does not mean that you need to be friends with your daughter's friends. It does mean that you have *met* her friends, have talked with them at least a little, and ideally have at least some knowledge of their family.

There are several ways you can get to know your daughter's friends. If she has a friend over to your house, invite her to

stay for supper as early in the friendship as possible so that
both you and your wife have a chance to observe and become
acquainted.

As I've mentioned, I have coached a number of our daughters' softball teams, and I have gotten to know a number of
their friends this way. There have been occasions when I was
unable to coach, but even then I helped out some and that also
gave me an opportunity to see and interact with a wide variety
of our daughters' friends.

Driving your daughter and her friend to some event is also
a fairly good way to get to know something about her. (In this
day and age I would strongly caution against your driving
alone with a girl you do not know, if at all possible.) I routinely
try to talk to the new girl, asking about her family and other
surface-level information. Sometimes I have gained real in-
sight into a girl's character in an exchange over relatively superficial information.

We have found that having a "kid-friendly home" is a very
good way to ensure that Vickie and I have a good opportunity
to keep an appropriate eye on friendships. We certainly don't
need to hear every word that is whispered during an eight-
year-old's tea party or a fourteen-year-old's chatter, but just
having the friends spend at least some of the time in our home
has generally positive effects.

Don't be afraid to set standards of behavior for your daughter's friends—at least while they are in your home.

While a certain amount of tolerance is warranted, certain
behaviors, such as bad language, should be kindly but deci-
sively dealt with. If your children are mature enough to tell
their friends what the rules are, that probably works best. If
not, you do it.

Be wary of close friendships where there is no spiritual dimension.

I am tempted to say that your daughter should not develop close friendships with unbelievers. That is close to my position, but it misses the mark in two distinct ways.

First, even if your daughter's friend is a Christian, their relationship might never include any kind of spiritual discussion. Especially as your daughter passes the age of eleven or twelve, you should strongly encourage your daughter to make sure that she and her friend include a spiritual dimension in their relationship. Perhaps it will be as simple as agreeing to share prayer requests and pray for each other. Maybe they will study the Bible together. But some degree of spirituality should mark our very closest friendships.

Second, I think we would miss the mark if we never had close friendships with unbelievers. But I still believe that all of our close friendships should have a spiritual dimension. If your daughter has a close friend who is an unbeliever, she should be encouraged to share the Gospel with this friend and to make sure that she regularly brings up spiritual matters in the course of their talks. Close friendships of this kind should regularly involve planting seed that may blossom into salvation in due season.

Gratuitous, negative comments about your daughter's friends are not very helpful.

This is a lesson I recently learned the hard way.

My daughter Katie told me about some last-minute changes in her basketball team's schedule. I brusquely said that I thought these schedule changes were not being handled properly by the people in charge—who were her friends. Katie took my comments to be derogatory about her friends. She felt compelled to defend her friends in the face of my accusatory comments.

Although my intent was to be protective of Katie, it actually came across as an unsolicited attack on her buddies. Katie's feelings were understandably hurt, and I created a situation where I unnecessarily set up a conflict of loyalties.

There are times when you have no choice but to make negative comments about your daughter's friends. But make sure of your facts. And it's also helpful to learn the fine art of *constructive criticism.* For instance, "Mary has a lot going for her—but I'd be happier for her to be your friend if she wasn't cutting down other people all the time. Maybe you could encourage her to be more positive and focus on the good things in other people."

If you start making accusations about your daughter's friends with your "verbal guns" blazing, you are likely to have an explosion on your hands. I know from experience that when I calmly make accurate and necessary constructive criticisms, I rarely engender a negative reaction in my girls. But generally I have found that Thumper's advice (in the movie *Bambi*) is good advice for a father: "If you can't say sumthin' nice, don't say anythin' at all."

Strongly encourage friendships among your own children.

One of my saddest memories from my teenage years was an occasion when I made some disparaging comments about having my little brother hanging around. I wanted to be with my friends. It really hurt my brother's feelings.

I have no idea who those friends were now. And since I never regularly see any of my friends from high school, I know for a fact that I have far more interactions with my brother than I do with whoever those "all-important" friends were.

Our three oldest girls have extraordinarily close relationships with one another. Our second "generation" of girls seems to be following a similar pattern to that of their older sisters.

In each of the trios, the older two girls are the closest. There is some tendency for the third child in each trio to be the "odd one out." It is very important for these third daughters to be accepted by her two immediately older sisters. It is a little tougher when they are young. Age differences tend to disappear as they get into their teens.

Despite these challenges, if you arrange your children's lives in a manner that encourages sibling friendships, they will be the deepest and best friendships they will ever have.

Our girls have always shared rooms. And being home schooled they spend a lot of time together. However, their recreational hours are often spent separately. If your daughters attend a conventional school in a manner that separates them, you may want to try to arrange their recreational activities to be done together. Sibling friendships are not likely to grow if they never spend meaningful time with each other.

Friendships made in childhood may or may not last for a lifetime. But *friendship skills* do last forever. A daughter who is trained to find her closest friends from those who share her moral and spiritual commitments will as an adult surround herself with friends who help her grow in faith.

And if she is trained to understand the importance of wise friendships, when she is grown and you aren't readily available, she'll know how to discern the difference between a "hometown talk-show host" dispensing worldly nonsense and the wise friendship of a real woman of God.

For Thought and Discussion

1. Have you taken appropriate steps to get to know your daughter's friends? What could you do to make your home more "kid friendly"?
2. Do you have spiritual and moral standards for your own close friendships? Does your daughter see you practicing what you preach?

3. Remember that even Christian girls may ignore God in the
   context of their friendships. What could you do to encourage your daughter to ensure that there is some spiritual interaction between her and her Christian friends?

6

Heels and Hose . . . and Beyond

The subject of "grown-up" attire and makeup may not seem like a big deal to you. But I *guarantee* you, it is a very big deal to your daughter. And it is a subject that you as a father need to interact with. Don't heap it all on your wife's shoulders. And don't be so bullheaded or tyrannical that you try to make these decisions on your own—without your wife.

Around age eleven or twelve, your daughter will begin a process that will change her from a child into an adult. She will think that she's an adult long before you will. But the choices she makes in these transition years—including choices about attire and makeup—will set the stage for what kind of an adult she will become. And it's important to remember that clothing and makeup can often be used to communicate a message. What's on the outside can often reflect what's on the inside. This is a lesson that you'll want your daughter to understand now and throughout her life.

A teenager who is taught a balanced view of attractiveness will grow into a woman who is comfortable with her own looks without becoming vain and self-centered on the one hand, or self-loathing and depressed about her appearance on the other. A teenager who is taught that outward appearance reflects inward reality won't grow into a woman who gives the impression of being constantly "on-the-make."

What's My Worth?

Though you value your daughter as your child, a teenage girl's self-esteem is largely wrapped up in her appearance. I'll never forget a conversation I had with the girl who was our high school Homecoming queen. She was, obviously, a very beautiful girl, but she told me that she didn't fully like the way she looked because she was "too thin." Her search for approval led her into a relationship with an older guy that left her pregnant before graduation.

Physical appearance is important to your daughter. And makeup and heels and hose and all of those things are an important and practical part of her appearance. But as you discuss the practical issues of "grown-up attire," remember that you are dealing with an issue that will influence her for life in terms of both her self-acceptance and her moral behavior. There's a lot of symbolism packed into a tube of lipstick, but make no mistake, these "small" practical issues have a very big meaning to your daughter.

For those who are looking for a definitive dress code, you are certainly aware that the Bible doesn't say precisely what age your daughter should be allowed to wear high heels. Or makeup. Or earrings. Therefore, where the Bible is silent, we cannot pretend there is a one-size-fits-all answer for every family. Your family should establish its own standards for these issues. I will tell you what our standards are for each of these areas, and for some that may be helpful. More importantly, I'll describe the *process* we used in establishing our standards. But keep in mind that our family's standards are nothing more than a suggestion or a single example.

Let's first identify the major issues you need to be aware of:

High heels
Hose
Makeup
Earrings and jewelry
Swimsuits
Hem length

Here are the Farris family standards for each of these topics:

High heels:	Age twelve (short heels); age fourteen (full heels).
Hose:	Age twelve (Attention dads: this involves shaving her legs, which is a big deal to girls.)
Makeup:	Age thirteen (a little); age fourteen (a moderate amount).
Pierced ears:	Age eighteen (clip earrings are okay younger).
Swimsuits:	Modest one-piece suits.
Hem length:	Not very far above the knee.

Let's quickly consider a few principles.

1. If you have more than one daughter, pick a standard wisely and do not change it lightly.

We had some major contentions when my wife and I started to loosen our standards up a bit with our third daughter, Katie. Christy and Jayme both were really upset that we intended to allow Katie to do things at a younger age. And if we went the other way and changed the standard to an older age, I know that we would have had an upset Katie on our hands.

One rule of thumb that can work: At what age was your wife allowed to do each of these things? If the answer to that question results in too young an age, you might ask your wife's mother when she was allowed to "dress grown-up." Generally speaking, the standards of the 1950s and early 1960s for most families were pretty well balanced and appropriately protective of younger girls, with maybe the exception of very liberal families.

As we approach the end of this century, I think most Christian dads would agree that the world has gone over the cliff in this area. If you have any doubt about it, go to a restaurant where high school couples are coming to dinner on prom night. Most of the guys look like the geeks we were in high school. Most of the girls in their prom dresses look like twenty-two-year-old sex bombs.

My point is this: *Don't let the world set your standards.* Talk it over with your wife. Pick a standard. Stick with it. Be consistent with each of your daughters.

Your goal is to develop a lifetime habit that ensures that her inner sense of beauty and attractiveness is not set by those who don't share her moral code. She should know that you genuinely believe that she is beautiful just the way God made her. And that you will cooperate with her to establish patterns that she likes, and which reflect favorably on Whose she is.

2. Don't let your daughter dress up in a way that materially overstates her age.

I was a beach lifeguard for the two summers before I was married. My fellow guards and I had a "bikini rule" to figure out how old a girl on our beach was. It went like this: "Look at the bikini. Guess how old she is. Subtract three years."

There were thirteen- and fourteen-year-old girls on our beach who were attracting the attention of guys who were eighteen, nineteen, and twenty. That is not a situation that any dad wants for his daughter. If a girl overstates her age by the way she dresses, she is inviting trouble from older guys.

Actually, makeup will probably overstate a girl's age more than any other single "dress-up" item. Young teenagers should use it sparingly, lest they be confused with much older girls.

Remember the overall purpose of makeup is to "look attractive." By definition, "attractive" involves attracting people. If you're like me, you tend to think that these "alleged people" your daughter may attract are in reality "slimy punks". . . who are as disgusting as you and I were at that age. (On the other hand, these young guys bear the burden of proving otherwise!)

Pick standards that encourage your daughter to look her age. It's okay to look pretty, but not too old.

A girl who looks too old when she is in her early teens can experience many lifelong consequences. First, she can get into real physical trouble today by attracting older and inappropriate guys. And second, she may well develop habits that may portray a risque image all her life. She may be driven to try to look and act as if she were twenty-one all her life. A life of hurt is the inherent result of such a fruitless effort.

3. Let your daughter pick her own style.

I hate to admit it, but I have a daughter who wears army boots. Or at least they kind of look that way to me. Our second daughter loves long, flowing dresses that have a very dramatic flair. I wouldn't have picked them out initially, but they really do look good on her. Our third daughter likes relatively baggy corduroy pants and slightly oversized plaid shirts for her casual clothes. I think this style looks like a lumberjack who needs to eat more often. But there is nothing immodest about any of these clothing tastes. And they are certainly not nearly as hideous as the orange polyester leisure suit I wore in the 1970s. (Believe it or not I actually wore it to court. And—I am telling you the truth—that day the judge had a bright green leisure suit on under his robe.)

I have recently decided that pure questions of taste—as opposed to modesty or symbols of rebellion, such as only wearing black, festooned with skulls and crossbones—are not worth battling over.

For instance, I'm not particularly fond of pierced ears. But ordinary pierced earrings are a matter of taste. And when our girls are old enough, they can make their own choice of taste. But piercing one's nose or eyebrow is out in our family.

When I have talked with our girls about these issues, my goal has been to do more than merely communicate my feelings about pierced eyebrows. I want them to understand that when they are grown and gone there will be some issues of taste and some issues of moral character that are reflected in their choices. It is my earnest desire that as adults they will be able to discern these distinctions and choose wisely even when the specific issue is no longer earrings.

4. Talking nicely has more positive impact than put-downs and yelling.

If you find that you want to draw a line that your daughter doesn't like—especially about an issue of clothing and modesty, you should be firm. Be warned: *Sarcastic comments at this point will be especially damaging.* Don't ever say something as stupid as, "You look like a lumberjack that needs to eat more often." Or, more seriously, a comment like, "You look like a hooker." These are destructive, unwarranted, and will bring the relationship with your daughter to an all-time low. Instead, use constructive criticism and say something like, "I don't think that outfit meets our standards of modesty. Why don't you wear your jean dress instead? It looks so good on you."

As in other areas of life, we want to use every opportunity to train our daughters how to seek and accept wise counsel and helpful and constructive criticism. We don't want to create high-strung, angry women who resist authority and resent males just because we were brutish fathers who couldn't understand their natural desire to "try on" new labels and find a style they liked.

The goal is to raise young women who will seek our godly advice throughout their lives because bonds of trust have been forged forever. Your interest and opinion about her looks not only *matter*—they are the most powerful tools you have for the beginning of a lifelong mentoring relationship with your daughter. If she trusts that you are *for* her, she will always come back for your opinion.

Someday all of our girls will dress very stylishly and look like their gorgeous mother. And for church and other similar occasions they already look just fine. (Well, almost always.) But when they dress in ways that are different than my adult tastes, I guess they are just proving that they are not really grown-up after all. Relish their growing-up time while they're finding their own style. Remember, they will be truly grown and gone all too soon.

For Thought and Discussion

1. Does the way you look at women when you are in the shopping mall—or on the beach—give your daughter the wrong signals about what's important in her appearance?
2. Have you taken the time to sit down with your wife and establish practical standards for your daughter *prior* to the time a decision has to be made so you're not creating "last-minute" standards without reasoning?
3. Do you communicate both an acceptance of your daughter's looks as given by God as well as a willingness to let her appropriately maximize her attractiveness?

Solving the Feminist Paradox

As a dad, I want my daughters to be all they can be. As a conservative, I don't want my daughters to be taken in by the arguments and schemes of the radical feminists.

In my political life, I have faced off with some of the best-known feminist icons of our day—Geraldine Ferraro and *MS.* magazine, just to name two. These left-wingers can't believe that I want to raise very competent daughters while rejecting their feminist ideologies.

At the heart of radical feminism is the view that men are evil and irrelevant. I'll always remember a feminist bumper sticker I saw in the early 1970s when I was in college: "A woman without a man is like a fish without a bicycle."

Feminists love to bash men. But ironically they seem to place an extraordinarily high priority on becoming just like men. Some want to dress like men, hold "male" jobs, and blur all distinctions between men and women in personal relationships. Lesbianism is considered by many to be the apex of feminism—proof that a man is truly irrelevant. Much feminist thinking has even invaded the Church.

Feminists do not use their most radical arguments as the "bait" to draw women into their movement. They use sensible arguments with just a subtle twist or two.

They point out that women earn, on average, about fifty-eight percent of what men earn. Then they argue that women should earn equal pay for equal work. But they ignore very real reasons for this phenomenon, like the fact that men collectively have more seniority because they do not take time out from their careers to bear children. When men and women are truly equally situated, the law currently enforces a rule demanding equal treatment. Because of media bias, they are allowed to make their arguments unanswered, and they do sound very appealing on the surface.

Girls are constantly exposed to these arguments on a daily basis in school. Any girl who reads a steady diet of public school textbooks will have a deep indoctrination into feminist thinking by the time she emerges from high school.

In the church, "evangelical feminism" is given a lot of ammunition by some of the excesses and abuses of some traditionalist teaching—and let's face it, there have been abuses. The Bible correctly teaches that a woman should be submissive to her husband. But "submission" has been translated by some into *subservience*, and has pushed some women into a place where they have no voice at all and little importance in certain churches and in many homes.

I believe the Bible clearly teaches that there are different roles in both the home and the church for men and women. But it does *not* teach that women are second-class citizens. Unfortunately, many Christian women and girls have good reason to be tempted by feminist ideology when they are treated as second-class citizens—especially when such disparate treatment comes in their own homes or churches.

Even the man who is not as biblically conservative can have a second-class view of women and their work. As one of our county officials said during a teachers' strike, "What do they want more money for? It's just a bunch of women teaching a bunch of kids!" The challenge for all of us as fathers is: *How do we raise our daughters to embrace their God-given feminine distinctiveness without engendering a feeling of being a second-class citizen?*

Our two oldest daughters really like the term "Empowered Traditionalist." They think it fits them perfectly. We have two very confident, self-assured young ladies who are quite capable of carrying on a successful career in the working world, but who desire to marry and be *stay-at-home* moms with the primary mission of raising children. They want to be living lives of significance, and they know that motherhood is likely to be the major portion of that significance. But they also are prepared and desire to demonstrate their significance in other areas of life as well.

How did this happen? Vickie and I recently tried to assess what we did to bring Christy and Jayme to this point in their lives. It is fairly easy to observe *what* has happened. Explaining *why* it happened is a bit tougher. But I believe there are three key points that I can share from our experience.

1. Treat your daughter like she has a brain.

Your daughter needs to feel like her life is both purposeful and valuable. And there is nothing that denigrates both purpose and value more than a feeling of stupidity—the "I'm Too Dumb Syndrome."

You treat your daughter like she has a brain when you give her a job and tell her she is capable to complete the task successfully. You engender feelings of stupidity when you give her a job . . . and then give her verbal and nonverbal clues that you expect her to fail.

If you supervise people at work, you will understand what I am about to say. You give an assignment to someone you *ex-*

pect to succeed in a much different manner than you give an assignment to a person about whose ability to succeed you entertain doubts. Most people who receive assignments from their boss can easily interpret the signals. They know if the boss trusts them or doesn't trust them by the way he or she communicates the assignment. Some bosses seem not to trust anyone, and they treat every employee as an imbecile.

There are basically three alternatives that you have as a father when you are interacting with your daughter: (1) You can demand perfection; (2) you can anticipate failure; or (3) you can expect success. Your daughter will know the difference between "a demand for perfection" and "an expectation of success" in the way you react to a completed task.

Let's say you give your daughter the assignment to clean your car, and everything looks great except for the hubcaps. If you say, "Thanks. Looks pretty good, generally. But don't you know that the hubcaps are a part of the car?" Such a comment is going to engender a feeling of stupidity. You have to handle such a situation very carefully. Sometimes it is simply best to let the less-than-perfect job pass. After all, if she is ten or twelve years old and you have given her a new or very challenging task, she probably has done it the best she can for her age. If it is appropriate or necessary to deal with the imperfections—and oftentimes it is—be sure to *reinforce the positive things she has done*. Treat the negatives as a reason to give more *training*, and not as proof that she is "a dumb girl."

I am a firm believer in giving my daughters very serious responsibilities. Christy was the deputy press secretary for my campaign for lieutenant governor. She had the daily responsibility to interact with the Washington *Post*, Washington *Times*, and other major newspapers in our state. She also had to juggle interview requests from Connie Chung at the national level to local radio reporters on tiny, rural stations. Jayme is now the chief graphic artist for our organization, Home School Legal Defense Association. I regularly give her design responsibilities by telling her a rough concept—and most often she comes back with a wonderful finished product. Both Christy and Jayme have proven that they can carry very significant adult-level responsibilities.

We didn't start out with these levels of responsibility. They started with chores that were maybe a little above their level—but not much. We gave them child-care responsibility early on (not alone, of course, until they were of a suitable age). Vickie taught them to cook when they were quite young. Since we home schooled our girls, we also gave them school assignments and communicated that we believed they would succeed. We tried to regularly praise them for their success.

Challenging assignments. Increasing levels of trust. Anticipated success. Praise. These are key factors in proving that you believe your daughter has a brain.

2. Guide your daughter to a vision for her life that embraces her femininity.

If you push your daughter toward a career as her first priority, she may have a difficult time embracing motherhood. If she has children one day, she may carry the depressive tendency to think, "Dad always wanted me to be a doctor, and look at me. I'm *just* a housewife and mother." Or, if you constantly communicate the idea that her sole destiny is to be a wife and mother—you may undermine her ability to accomplish other important goals that God has for her. Also, she may end up *neither* a wife nor a mother, and be left having to negotiate through some tough emotional problems if this lifelong "vision" is never fulfilled.

Vickie and I tell our girls no one—not a man or a woman—should try to "have it all." No person is capable of having more than one "top priority" in his or her life. We believe that a *mother's* top priority belongs to her children. But there is a marked distinction between a "top priority" and a "sole priority."

Communicate to your teenage daughters that college and

ultimate career plans need to be viewed in light of the full range of priorities that may face a woman one day—like motherhood. Personally, we encourage our girls to look at careers that can be done *part-time* from home while they are being loving, *full-time* moms.

For instance, Christy is well underway in her training to become a political journalist. It's something she can do either on a full-time basis in an office, or part-time from home.

At the ripe old age of eighteen, Jayme is a great graphic artist and a very good editor. Likewise, she can one day pursue these related professions part-time in an office at home when and if she becomes a mom.

Both of these professions are something that can be started and stopped throughout their life when motherhood demands more of their time.

Part of this puzzle is finding a career that makes sense to pursue on a part-time basis at home. But another part is instilling a sense of importance for being a stay-at-home mom, should the Lord bless your daughter with children. The key to creating that desire, I believe, is found in the third factor.

3. Treating your wife with dignity and value is the most important way to encourage your daughter to embrace the God-given gift of motherhood.

Perhaps the most important reason our girls have a vision for a traditional role as a wife and mother is that they look at Vickie *and they like what they see.*

Your wife is going to play an extremely important role in creating the right vision for your daughter. *But your relationship to your wife—whether or not you treat her with respect—is of enormous importance.*

The world treats "men's work" as a truly worthwhile endeavor. You are the representative of "men's work" in your family. If you act as if your role is far more important than the role played by your at-home wife, don't be surprised when your daughter rejects family life later and wants *your* role on the job instead.

There are at least four aspects of my relationship with Vickie that I think have helped our daughters come to the point where they have the vision for their potential future roles as wives and mothers.

I never make major decisions in my life without Vickie's enthusiastic agreement—and the girls know it. For more than twenty years people have tried to get me to run for political office. It is a subject that has been talked about in our house ever since our children were born. Our girls know that every time I was asked to consider a particular office, I would talk it over thoroughly with Vickie. They also know that if Vickie expressed reservations or doubts, my answer would be "no."

They have also seen this same process of mutual decision-making in other major areas—buying a home, making moves, career choices—and not-so-major decisions like paint colors and wallpaper patterns.

The Bible teaches that husbands are ultimately responsible for family decisions. But woe to that husband who does not consult with his wife, and who does not treat her views as tantamount to veto power. Certainly there will arise a time when you have to make a decision contrary to your wife's position. Such a move should be an exception and done with great hesitation and gentleness.

As important as it is for me to consult with Vickie on major decisions and to follow her counsel initially, it is even more important that I don't bad-mouth the decision after-the-fact. If my girls heard me second-guessing a jointly made decision, saying, for example, "If only your mother hadn't said *no* we could be living in that great new house across town"—it would undermine everything.

As our girls have gotten older, I have included them in the circle of counsel I seek for major decisions in my life. I not only value their observations, but asking their opinion has the secondary benefit of training them to understand that their future role as a counselor to their husband is of great value.

Our girls have seen me "yield the right of way" to my wife's calling and vision for her life. Vickie, as you've gathered by now, is a home-schooling mother of nine children. When we were dating I won a college speech and debate contest advocating "zero population growth." Having a large family has been basically my wife's idea—which only goes to prove that she is a better debater than I am.

Our girls are aware of this dynamic in our relationship. They know that their mom has convinced me to have a large family *and they understand that Vickie believes that raising godly children is her primary mission for God in life.*

What I say about this is very important to my girls. If I complain about having a large family after having gone along with each child's creation, I would send very damaging signals. I simply cannot say things like, "If we weren't having another baby we could afford to send you to a better college." Or, "Because we have so many kids we have to drive an '89 Dodge fifteen-passenger van, rather than a '96 Dodge Viper."

There is no question that Vickie's vision for her life has at times created some conflicts with the things I would like to do. As I mentioned earlier, I had every intention to run for the United States Senate in 1996. Without any pressure from Vickie, I decided not to run because we have a lot of young children. Looking at this decision from one perspective, some might say, "Your wife's vision for her life got in the way of your vision for your life." I reject such a thought. I want my girls to know the value I place upon their mother's vision for her life. Also, verbalizing such a thought would make my youngest children feel like their very existence is a hindrance to me.

As we have discussed this topic as a family, I have been careful to embrace our commitment to a large family and let them know that I know that God's plan for my future includes all of them.

I don't want to leave the impression that this is all one-sided and that I only give way to Vickie. She yields a great deal in deference to the calling that God has placed on my life. After all, she enthusiastically backed my effort to run for the part-time job of lieutenant governor. For a number of years, I have done a lot of speaking at conferences. I am encouraged but certainly not required to do such speaking as a part of my job. Vickie could say, "Three conferences a year. That's it. I need you at home." She doesn't do that. We have an agreed limit, but it is very generous in light of the tremendous responsibilities that Vickie has to shoulder when I am away. It is important that my daughters (and my sons) see a balance. The truth is that we yield to each other and show deference to the callings that each of us has received from God for our lives.

It's not just the big things. It is almost as important that I show deference to my wife in day-to-day activities. If I always "do my own thing" (for which I have a great propensity) rather than showing an appropriate degree of helpfulness around the home, I communicate to my daughters that Vickie's work is not as important as mine. I struggle to some degree in this area, but I try to communicate in word and in deed that I think that "Vickie's work" is important and valuable.

One of the most important dynamics in our family life is our home schooling. Before we began to home school, Vickie used to wistfully say things like, "I wonder if I should get a job rather than just sit around here all day wiping up spills and changing diapers." Vickie graduated number two in her high school class, and before she began to teach our children she missed intellectual stimulation at times. But despite these momentary thoughts, she remained committed to her role as full-time mom.

When we started home schooling, the dynamic changed. She was now involved in academic instruction—a task the world about us greatly values. She had plenty of intellectual stimulation and plenty of perceived value for her life.

I am not trying to say that home schooling is the only way for a *stay-at-home* mom to have real value in her role. I was not home schooled and my own stay-at-home mother played a great role in my life. What I am saying is that home schooling is something that has been very helpful to my wife to bring her a vision for her femininity in which she finds fullness and purpose. Our girls see this vision. They embrace this vision modeled by their mother. And it is my job to support this vision enthusiastically.

I talk to Vickie in a way that respects her intelligence. I treat Vickie like she has a brain, not the way I see some men treat their wives.

Your daughters see more about your relationship with your wife than either of you would probably like. No matter who you are, you are going to make some mistakes in the way you communicate with your wife in front of your children. The important thing is that your normal communication is respectful, and that violations of this rule are rare.

Sarcasm is probably the number one way that men communicate the "you dummy" attitude to their wives. Too many men make redneck comments that communicate, "Shut up, woman."

Your wife does not have to be an intellectual giant—or understand economics, politics, or the Internet—to possess compassion and great wisdom. Talk to her *respectfully*, and your daughters will receive positive reinforcement as well.

I tell my daughters in plain language that their mother's role is important. While actions speak louder than words, words are important, too.

From time to time my girls hear me praise my wife for the valuable role she plays in our family. They will hear me say, "You have done a great job teaching algebra to Katie this year. I know it hasn't been easy, but it was important for her to learn." And at other times I tell the girls more directly that I think what their mom does is valuable. I'll say something like, "Jessica, your mom sacrifices a lot of her time to prepare lessons for you. You need to give them your best effort." They also hear me make such comments in public and in writing. If I didn't say the same thing at home, the public comments would be hypocrisy and would create bitterness. A consistent message of praise for my wife and her role as a mother is an extremely important factor in helping our girls to enthusiastically embrace her role as their first choice for their long-range future.

Feminists prey on daughters of under-appreciated mothers. Show appreciation and give value to your wife. Your daughters, too, will become "Empowered Traditionalists."

For Thought and Discussion

1. Do you treat your wife or daughter in a condescending manner? In what ways do you think a male-bashing attitude might start to look attractive as a result of your words and actions?
2. Do you talk as if motherhood is every bit as important as your career? If not, what effect do you think this will have on your daughter in the future and your wife today?
3. How can you expose your daughter to some career opportunities that can potentially be done from her home?

Responsible Young Women

I once had a secretary, "Carrie," who was generally very good at almost everything. But she had one major flaw. She simply wouldn't get to work on time. She was supposed to arrive at 8:30, but she always would sneak in a few minutes before nine. In desperation, I changed her starting time to nine and moved back quitting time accordingly. She started arriving closer to 9:30. Eventually I imposed an ultimatum: if she accumulated sixty minutes of tardiness, she would be fired. She quit just a few days later because she realized she just couldn't make herself arrive on time.

Arriving on time was a small part of Carrie's duties. But her failure to be faithful in that small thing prohibited her from proving her faithfulness in the larger areas of responsibility.

Without reservation I can say that our girls—all six of them—are hard-working young ladies who can handle serious responsibilities far beyond their years.

Christy and Jayme have both held full-time, very responsible jobs. As I write this section Jayme is away from home after a full-day's work as a graphic artist, finishing the typesetting and artwork for a twenty-page magazine on presidential candidates. She'll be home around midnight.

Both of our oldest girls saved enough money to pay cash for their own cars. Christy also saved enough to pay for half of her own college expenses for the bulk of her first two years in school.

I am fully confident of the abilities of our oldest two girls (and Katie, our third oldest, is right on their heels) to manage a family. My wife and I have no hesitancy leaving the oldest girls in charge of our family while we are out of town.

Jessica and Angie are terrific helps around the home. By the time they are "safe" baby-sitting age, they will be over-qualified for such duties.

Neither Vickie nor I can say that we set out in an organized fashion to train our girls to be able to function at an unusually high level of responsibility. But certain requirements helped our girls develop strong habits in this area. Though we stumbled our way through and to good results, maybe you can do them on purpose. Our basic guide was the lesson that my secretary, Carrie, needed to hear: *Be faithful in small things and you will get a chance to prove yourself faithful in greater things.*

Work and Responsibility

As I've said, when you have a family of nine children, you have no choice. All of your children have to learn to work hard. Between Vickie and me, my childhood prepared me much better for the work that we have encountered with our extra-large family.

My mother was one of eleven. During the latter years of the depression when she was a young teenager, her whole family followed the pattern of migrant workers that was made so famous in *The Grapes of Wrath*. My father is the oldest of five children. He grew up in the heart of the depression on a rocky farm in the middle of the Ozarks in Arkansas. His father, my grandfather, was not the most diligent worker, and the responsibility for the family fell considerably on my father's shoulders.

I was one of four—the second child, the oldest son. Let me say that my sisters, brother, and I were required to work very hard as children. We picked fruit in the summer. We did substantial chores all year long. I painted, I mowed, and we dug up the whole yard to remove quackgrass—twice. I helped my dad dig a drywell system by hand. I dug a 100-foot-long irrigation ditch. I hated it. I wanted to goof off. But I had no choice. It was required. It was expected. My parents constantly reminded us that it was a whole lot easier for us than it had been on them in their childhood. And they were right.

Vickie, on the other hand, was an only child. She was expected to keep her room clean. She had a few light household chores, but for the most part she was expected to concentrate her hard work on her academic studies. And she did, graduating as salutatorian of her class. Vickie says that she has a hard time compelling our girls to work because she didn't have nearly as much to do when she was a girl. But we all realize the absolute necessity of mutual efforts to keep our family moving. And so our girls work. And I constantly remind them that I had it harder when I was a child. (I exaggerate a good deal.)

We stumbled into a lot of the principles that child-training experts recommend. What we can tell you is that these principles work.

Principle 1: Give your daughter serious responsibilities and expect her to work hard.

There is no question about the value of the hard work that our girls have been required to undertake. And frankly, the lesson to be learned is pretty straightforward. Give your girls real opportunities to work and they are much more likely to be able to shoulder and balance substantial responsibilities later. And you don't have to have nine children to make this happen. An only daughter can be trained to grow in responsibilities if you decide to pursue that path.

Hard work for a five-year-old can be as simple as picking up her things (three or four times a day), making her bed, helping to clean the table, helping to pick up the mess made by your toddler, and feeding pets.

A ten-year-old can be expected to wash dishes, fold wash, keep her room clean, watch younger children (with an adult in the house), help with simple cooking, help Dad pick up the yard prior to mowing, help weed the garden, and, of course, keep her own room clean.

I don't want anyone to believe that our girls have never had time to play. They play several hours each day in their younger years (below age twelve) and have plenty of time for recreation and activities during their teens.

Principle 2: Nuke the tube.

One of the main reasons that they have so much time for substantial work (including schoolwork) and substantial play is that our children watch very little television. We have actually relaxed our time constraints in the last few years and allow about four or five hours per week of television shows. Some studies show that the average child in America watches approximately three and a half to four hours of television a day. Twenty-five percent of all children watch from four and a half to eleven hours of television a day.

A child who sits in front of a television is not learning to work, play, or read. Working, playing, and reading are purposeful activities for children.

If you can't control your own television habits (my wife watches no television, and I watch a sports event every couple weeks), don't expect your girls to curb themselves. You have to set a good example.

If you are one of these people who simply cannot control themselves with a TV, throw the stupid thing away. It is better to never see the news than to allow your bad habits to turn your daughters into video vegetables.

Principle 3: Give the job to the youngest child capable of doing it and keep increasing levels of responsibility.

We have a big dog. One hundred and twenty pounds. He demands to be fed. We used to rotate feeding duty between our three "middle" children. But we discovered that our two "middle" daughters could fold wash, and that Michael (our oldest son) couldn't fold wash. Michael is now the permanent dog feeder (until Emily is old enough to share the responsibility).

By giving each chore assignment to the youngest child capable of assuming the job, you provide a way to ease the work load on an older child (which helps prevent resentment). And it has the tremendous advantage of pushing your children to greater and greater levels of responsibility.

Principle 4: Provide rewards for extra effort.

It is our philosophy that children should do a certain amount of work in order to share in the responsibility that goes with belonging to a family. If a child will not work, neither shall she have privileges. (It's only a slight modification of 2 Thessalonians 3:10.)

However, I think it is very important, too, for our daughters to learn the connection between work and money. In our family, extra work produces money. If our toddlers have made a mess in the basement, we have to ask our middle (and sometimes our older) children to clean it up. If it is especially messy, or if just one or two children have to clean it up, we will pay them a dollar or so for tackling a job that requires a lot of extra effort.

I especially like to provide small rewards (fifty cents to a dollar) when one of our daughters takes initiative to do a job without being asked. A ten-year-old who is trained by encouragement and rewards to see a mess the baby has made and clean up the mess without being asked, may someday have the initiative and capacity to be the CEO of a Fortune 500 company. Hard work and initiative are so rare these days, a little training and encouragement in this area can produce far greater results than you might imagine.

Responsibility With Money

Principle 1: Teach your daughter that money comes from work.

We touched on this principle in the work section, but it bears emphasis.

Many families raise children with the same discredited philosophy that is destroying the finances of the federal government: *entitlements.* Children who believe that they are entitled to receive all their wants and desires will develop the tastes to be top executives, but will demonstrate the work habits of the habitually unemployed.

Even in the most affluent families, children need to have certain things that they cannot get unless they work for them.

Our middle daughters have developed a real interest in the American Girls doll collection. These are of good quality but fairly expensive. Jessica just asked me if she could order a free item called "The Savings Game." It is a booklet created by the Pleasant Company, which manufactures American Girl dolls, with some stickers to teach girls how to create a work-and-savings plan to allow them to save up enough money to buy the items they want. This is a tremendously valuable idea. We ordered two "free" savings plans. The company knows that teaching girls to save will in the long run sell more products, but I am glad they profit from this because teaching girls to sublimate their immediate desires to participate in a long-term work-and-savings plan is simply invaluable.

Principle 2: Teach your daughter to tithe.

This is not difficult to do. There are really only two things that are necessary. First, instruct your daughter that she needs to dedicate the first fruits of her labor to the Lord. Second, model the desired behavior.

The Garvises, a family in our church with five daughters and one infant son, recently demonstrated a tremendous lesson in giving. Their mother encouraged the girls to set up a popsicle stand this past summer. She advanced them the price of the first batch of popsicles, but she expected back her original investment. They sold quite a number of popsicles and made a good profit by summer's end.

From the very beginning, these girls had taken on this whole project with the goal to give away all of their profits to a missionary—a single woman who was going to work in a secular job in an Islamic country as a means of reaching Islamic women for Christ. Their mother arranged for this gift to be given by the girls (ages five to eleven) to the missionary in front of the entire church. You could see the sparkle in these girls' eyes as they saw the tangible results of their labors being used for God.

The normal practice should be to teach your daughter to tithe. But once in a while it wouldn't hurt to take on a special project and give all of the money to the Lord's work.

Principle 3: Teach your daughter that money should be spent carefully.

When my oldest daughters were about twelve or thirteen, they paid little attention to prices when we shopped for clothes. Dad always paid. They simply didn't care.

A funny thing happened when they started to earn enough of their own money to buy at least some of their own clothing. Not only were they careful with their money, they were more careful and prudent with mine. When they were responsible for earning and spending their own money, they learned the value of careful purchasing.

I do the majority of the grocery shopping for our family. I often take one of the children along. One of the things I try to do is to teach our daughters (and ultimately our sons) some principles of comparison shopping. I teach them to read unit-pricing labels so they can figure out which item is actually the cheapest. And then we talk about the variance in quality of products. They need to learn that the cheapest is not always the best value.

One practical shopping skill I learned from my dad that my girls have seen me apply very often is this: If there is a great sale price on an item that we use regularly, I often buy as much of it as the store will let me have. There is a certain laundry product that my wife uses a lot (nine kids, remember). I was buying a $3 bottle every couple weeks. But about eighteen months ago a local grocery store had a *two-for-the-price-of-one* special. I bought three cases of the stuff.

Principle 4: Teach your daughter to shoulder responsibility for her mistakes.

My best illustration of this principle comes from an example with my son, but the lesson is really gender-neutral, so bear with me. Michael decided to hide inside our stereo cabinet that was (notice the verb tense) covered with a glass door. He didn't seem to mind the fact that a two-year-old wouldn't have fit in the space. He was way too big, not to mention way out of line, to get inside that cabinet.

Needless to say the glass door shattered, but fortunately Michael was not hurt. There is no way that Michael could ever earn enough money from outside our family to pay for that door. Frankly, I haven't even tried to replace it. But I was going to make Michael pay to learn responsibility. We were about three weeks from going on vacation. He was required, under severe threats of restrictions while on vacation, to find fifty additional jobs he could volunteer to do and complete before we left on our trip. We had to push and cajole just a bit, but he was able to find and complete the required number of jobs.

I believe that both Michael and his sisters learned that if you break something through irresponsible behavior, you are going to pay. We never require our children to pay for things that are broken in the normal course of living (dropped glasses, etc.). But if they are goofing off or engaging in behavior that is considered irresponsible in light of their age and something is broken, they are going to have to work it off or pay it off. This teaches the need to take care of one's own things and to shoulder responsibility for damage done to others' things.

Principle 5: Teach your daughter to be totally honest.

When one of our older daughters was about five, we found out that she stole a candy bar from a grocery store. The Old Testament says that if a person steals a sheep, they have to pay back four sheep. And in Luke 19, Zacchaeus, the tax collector, offered to pay back four times the amount to anyone he had cheated. So we made this daughter go to the grocery store, tell the manager what she had done, and then offer to pay back four times the price of the candy bar from her own money.

She was such a cute little girl we thought that the manager would smile at her, accept only the actual price of the candy bar, and mildly encourage her to be honest in the future. We were prepared to insist that she pay back the fourfold fine.

We didn't have to worry. He not only took all the money she offered, he was extraordinarily harsh with her and seemed on the verge of calling the police. Even though he was rougher than we expected, it was actually the best for our daughter. She had a scary brush with authority, and this daughter has never done anything even slightly dishonest in the decade-plus that has followed.

There is no question about the best method of teaching financial honesty to your daughter. When you are going to the movies and your daughter gets in for two dollars less if she is under twelve, do you lie to save a couple bucks? When you are flying across the country and the airline requires your two-year-old to buy a ticket, do you tell your six-year-old, "Be sure and tell the flight attendant that Jenny is twenty months old. Don't say she is two"?

Your dishonesty will breed dishonesty in her. If you cheat on the little things, don't be surprised when you discover that your daughter is dishonest in some way you hold to be both significant and sacred.

Our goal as fathers is to raise daughters who are responsible when they are adults. Adult-like attitudes about money can be instilled throughout childhood.

My mother was raised in very difficult economic circumstances during the latter years of the depression. She was required to pick cotton in Texas in the winter, hoe lettuce in Colorado in the summer, and was able to attend school very sporadically.

She now owns two large Christian bookstores and has done very well financially because what she learned from her father was not to focus on the deprivation, but to work hard, use money responsibly . . . and to be totally honest in your dealings with people.

I want my girls to be like her. (Thanks, Mom!)

For Thought and Discussion

1. How often is the television on in your home? Is the TV the center of your family life or is your family? Have either you

or your daughter been made richer financially or spiritually by the amount of time you spend just watching?

2. What have you taught your daughter about tithing by verbal instruction? By your example?

3. What work can you give your daughter to begin teaching her responsibility? What rewards can you give her to teach her the proper value of money?

Raising Daughters
for the Future
of Our Nation

Zan Tyler is about five-two, just a slip of a woman. When she started walking the halls of the South Carolina legislature on behalf of home schoolers, the men who dominated the chamber thought little of her ability. But by persistence, and by demonstrating the ability to produce organized support from grassroots voters, Zan has become an influential fixture in South Carolina politics. The men who looked upon her grassroots, home-based activism with bemused indifference, now admire her or at least give her begrudging respect.

The political arena is where I live my professional life. And I can tell you firsthand the importance of having motivated women on your side in any political battle.

My examples in this chapter are going to seem much more involved than those experienced by normal dads. Nonetheless, men whose work keeps them focused in other arenas can raise daughters who know the rights and responsibilities of good citizenship.

First, let me tell you my perspective about the importance

of women in the guidance of our communities, states, and our nation.

I was twenty-six, only two years out of law school, when three women came to me and asked me to file one of the most important cases I have ever undertaken. They wanted me to challenge the constitutionality of the bill passed in Congress which gave the National Organization for Women and others an extra three years to get states to ratify the Equal Rights Amendment.

One of these three women was my fourth-grade Sunday school teacher. All of them were approximately my mother's age.

When they were through, they had convinced three state legislators to bring this challenge *and* convinced me to be the lawyer. When the case was over we—along with another team—had won.

Another time I was involved in a dispute about sexually graphic movies which were being shown in public high schools. A woman state senator asked me to find out which schools were using the movies, and so I tried to do so. I ended up in a court case with the state library over these public records.

As a result of this case, I was asked to speak to the national convention of the American Library Association—a gathering of over 4,000 in San Francisco. They wanted me to come to the convention so they could show the audience what a "real live censor" looked like. They clearly wanted me to make a fool of myself by coming and railing in heated terms against the evils in the schools.

Initially, I had every intention of living up to their expectations. But I was confronted with a completely different approach when I showed the draft of my speech to my wife, Vickie. With just a few words she made it clear to me that she thought that the speech was unduly harsh and that I would be made to look like a fool.

I completely rewrote the speech, taking a much more conciliatory tone while not backing off one inch in the substantive message. Vickie approved.

When I was done with the speech, I had a couple dozen librarians approach me in a happy throng. They said to me (in effect), "We are Christians and we were so afraid of what you were going to say here today. We thought that you would make all of us look foolish. But your speech was great. You stated our position in the very best possible way. Thank you so much."

The American Library Association was so impressed with the speech that they printed it in their journal. A publication of the American Bar Association picked it up and carried it in their journal. And I received numerous speaking invitations as a result of my revised speech.

Let me be clear: It was my wife who had the wisdom to get me to balance my passion for the *issues* with compassion for *people*.

For over six years, I served as the General Legal Counsel for Concerned Women for America—America's largest political organization for women. Beverly LaHaye is the founder and president of this fine pro-family organization. Consequently, I had the opportunity to watch Beverly and many of CWA's fine state and regional leaders do many, many important things in the political arena.

And when I ran for lieutenant governor of Virginia, I had dozens of women in my campaign in key positions of leadership and as advisers.

The net result of my experience in politics tells me that Christian women are absolutely vital to the efforts to take a nation back to its moral roots and Judeo-Christian heritage. I have seen women as leaders, advisers, and helpers. Without Christian women, our work to bring Christian spiritual principles to local, state, and national government will get nowhere.

Maggie Smeltzer

I have also seen the tremendous impact that girls—especially adolescent girls—can have on the political process. Perhaps the best example is Maggie Smeltzer.

Maggie attended a public school for the first couple years of her education. She was not doing very well. In fact, the school district considered her to be "borderline learning disabled." Her parents decided to home school her at that point to see if they could do better.

Under the former law in Pennsylvania, the school district had the power to approve or disapprove the Smeltzers' request to home school Maggie. Reluctantly, the district approved the request for two consecutive years.

After two years of home schooling, Maggie's test scores were now so high that she was considered "gifted and talented." When her parents sought permission for the third year of home schooling, the school district denied permission on the premise that these parents were incapable of teaching a gifted and talented child!

The district filed immediate criminal charges against the family, but I was able to get them dismissed with the threat of federal litigation.

A couple years later, the Pennsylvania legislature took up a bill to liberalize the home schooling law. Maggie, now about thirteen, was called to testify before a joint legislative committee. She was asked a number of questions, and the committee members sat in rapt attention as this thirteen-year-old girl gave great answers. Finally, she was asked, "Maggie, what do you want to do as a career?" She answered, "I want to be a constitutional litigator."

With that answer, the debate was over. Maggie had clearly trumped the opposition to this bill coming from the education establishment. And Pennsylvania is the only state to have ever passed a home school law with a unanimous affirmative vote in both houses.

Kid Power

Recently, my three oldest daughters and a half-dozen friends organized the "sign brigade" for a conservative woman candidate who was running for the chairman's position of our County Board of Supervisors. When I walked into the auditorium, it looked as if it were a rally for our candidate rather than an election contest between two people. The "sign war" had clearly been won by this group of teenagers.

Christy told me later, "I can always tell who is going to win a race by watching their 'sign team.' The losers always have a bunch of older women in business suits trying to tape up a few signs. The winners have a bunch of teenagers in jeans and tennis shoes who take the place by storm."

Incidently, Christy's candidate won that political convention in a narrow contest and went on to win a very close general election. Our daughters and their friends helped in the process of pushing a good woman to the top.

Our youngest three girls also have accompanied me to a number of political events. They learned to hand out *"I Like Mike"* stickers. Voters found it hard to resist a request to wear a political sticker from a blond little girl.

I have interacted with many dozens of ten- to eighteen-year-old girls who have played a role in a great variety of political activities. There are a number of observations I have made about these "activist" girls:

First, they have a great amount of fun. Political events have crowds, excitement, and a lot of purposeful work. Girls who are exposed to this kind of activity are given the opportunity to learn that positive, appropriate activities can really be enjoyable.

Second, girls who become personally involved in political activity when they are young normally develop a vision for involvement that lasts a lifetime. They are much more likely to understand the importance of politics and citizenship than someone who merely reads about these topics in books and magazines. When they are forty and there is a need for a mom to run for the school board, a woman who was an activist as a girl is far more likely to step forward and take on the challenge. An election is no mystery to her. She's been there and done that.

Third, girls who have been exposed to civic involvement are usually much better students in history and government courses than their non-active counterparts. A student who has some experience also develops context for information learned from a book. As in any subject area, a student with *experience* plus information will always do better than a student who has only information.

Fourth, I have observed that girls who are exposed to the give-and-take of real-life politics are much more capable in articulating their own views than those who have not been involved. My daughters have had numerous opportunities to see me and others state our positions orally and in writing. And they have seen the counterattacks from the other side. By this kind of exposure they learn what kind of arguments are convincing, and what kind are not nearly as convincing.

I have had dozens of women who have become active in politics later in life tell me, "I wish I would have paid attention more to my courses on history and government. It wasn't interesting in those days, but it is really interesting to me now." Activism is one of the best ways to bring these courses alive for your daughter.

If you want your daughter to be prepared to maximize her role as a citizen of this country, there are two categories of "know-how" that are important for you to consider. There are certain things "your daughter should know"—academic knowledge. And there are other things "she should know how to do"—practical knowledge.

Five Things Your Daughter Should Know to Be an Effective Citizen

1. Your daughter should know that active average citizens are the guarantors of freedom.

Only those who participate have any effect on making a difference in the battle for freedom in America. Thomas Jefferson said, "If once the people become inattentive to the public affairs, you and I and Congress and Assemblies, Judges and Governors, shall all become wolves."

It is important that neither you nor your daughter believe that it is necessary to be involved in politics at the level that my own life suggests. Law and politics are both my career and my calling. I have a unique vantage point that allows me to see the tremendous value that is offered in our system by the moms and dads, men and women, boys and girls who devote a few hours a month to making our nation a better place. Frank C. Ross has said it well, "The world is moved not only by the mighty shoves of the heroes, but also by the aggregate of the tiny pushes of each honest worker."

2. Your daughter should have an appreciation of the history of our nation.

Knowledge of American history is not the same as appreciation of our nation's history. Most of the current public school textbooks on American history are written with the perspective that our Founding Fathers were rich, white, religious hypocrites and not to be trusted. America's warts are magnified. America's heroes are stigmatized. Christianity is either ignored or equated with the likes of the Ku Klux Klan.

I would urge every Christian father to read *The Light and the Glory* by Peter Marshall and David Manuel[1] aloud to their children. This book tells the stories of early America that expose your children to at least two things which are very different from material they will ever get in most textbooks. First, this book meticulously demonstrates how the hand of God has been obvious throughout events that led to the foundation of our country. These stories are as exciting as many adventure novels. Second, this book will show how the founders of this nation were motivated by good hearts. They made mistakes, that is certain. Who doesn't? But heroes are men and women who have good hearts and who overcome their mistakes to accomplish great things.

David Barton's excellent video-tapes on America's Christian heritage are also well worth obtaining and watching.[2] Your children will be astonished to learn how much Christianity influenced America in a positive way. This kind of information will not only inoculate your children against the subversion that most history texts contain, but it will also turn them into warriors for the right cause.

3. Your daughter should understand the biblical foundation for civic and political involvement.

Most Christians who are of my generation were taught that Christians should not be involved in the dirty business of politics. And make no mistake about it. Politics *is* unquestionably a dirty business. But, we have responsibilities as Christian citizens to see to it that as the salt of the earth we do our very best to disinfect this dirty business.

Consider these four verses as a simple foundation to teach your daughter that political and civic involvement are *one* of the important (but secondary) duties of Christians.

Psalm 125:3: "The scepter of the wicked will not remain over the land allotted to the righteous, for then the righteous might use their hands to do evil."

This verse teaches us the consequences of allowing wicked people to rule over us. We are told that one of the results of such leaders is that God's people begin to fall and use their hands to do evil. I am convinced that one of the reasons we have seen so many famous (and not-so-famous) pastors and other Christians fall into sin and disgrace is because the judgment predicted in this verse has fallen on the house of God. We need good leaders if we want to ensure that we don't wander off and fall into active sin.

Ephesians 5:11: "Have nothing to do with the fruitless deeds of darkness, but rather expose them."

There is a popular liberal bumper sticker that reads: "If you oppose abortion—don't have one." That's good advice as far as it goes. However, this bumper sticker suggests that pro-lifers should not speak out when others have abortions. This inference is directly contrary to the teaching of this verse. Paul tells us that avoiding personal involvement in sin is only the first step in our responsibility as Christians. There is another important step as well. We are to "expose" sin. What I believe Paul means by this is that we are to make it known to the world that sinful behavior is wrong. I don't think this verse means we are supposed to go around uncovering every single sin that other people do and bringing it to public attention. I believe it means that we are to make sure the world knows the boundaries of right and wrong. We are to reinforce the collective conscience God has given to each member of the human family. It is our job to help people to know that abortion is the wrongful taking of the life of an innocent child.

Let me illustrate how important this instructional responsibility is with a personal example. When I was nineteen years old, the state of Washington had a ballot initiative for the people of the state to decide whether or not to legalize abortion—two years *prior* to *Roe* v. *Wade*. Even though I was raised in a very solid Baptist church, I received absolutely no instruction on this issue from my church. I had heard my parents say only two sentences to each other on the topic—literally two sentences. My dad said he thought it was okay, but my mom didn't. But neither of them could explain their reasoning.

I voted in favor of legalizing abortion as a born-again Christian in 1971. I say that to my own shame. (Incidently, today my parents, my childhood church, and I are all vigorously pro-life.)

When we fail to teach the world the rules of right and wrong, moral confusion is the result. I was confused in 1971 because I had not been taught where the boundaries were. Consequently, I voted the wrong way on a very important issue.

Daniel 4:27: (Daniel is speaking to King Belteshazzar) "Therefore, O king, be pleased to accept my advice: Renounce your sins by doing what is right, and your wickedness by being kind to the oppressed. It may be that then your prosperity will continue."

Social conservatives were told many times during the Reagan and Bush administrations, "We'll get to the social issues *after* we've dealt with the economic issues." The book of *Daniel* teaches us that this thinking is upside-down. If we want to see prosperity continue, we should deal first with our national wickedness. We should also ensure that kindness is extended to the oppressed. Prosperity will then pretty well take care of itself.

Proverbs 3:6: "In all your ways acknowledge him, and he will make your paths straight."

Those who argue that Christians shouldn't apply biblical principles to their lives as citizens have a difficult time overcoming this verse. All means all. If we are to acknowledge God in all our ways, it means that in our roles as citizens, we have to exercise that role in a way that acknowledges God. Acknowledging God means that He is in charge. If He is not in charge in that aspect of our lives, then we are saying that God is a Great Big Adviser—but that role falls short of being God. God by His very nature is in control of us. We have to be His kind of citizen or we fail to acknowledge Him as God in all our ways.

4. Your daughter should understand the practical workings of government.

Mechanical, book-oriented lessons about government processes are likely to be terribly boring—at least initially. I would encourage you to take your daughter to see your city council, school board, or county government in action. A trip to your State Capitol when the state legislature is in session is a very worthwhile endeavor. You might also want to watch Congress in action on C-Span.

If you go to the State Capitol, I would suggest that you do three things if at all possible: attend a committee hearing; watch both the House and Senate in action on the floor; and arrange a personal meeting with your own representative. Generally, your representative will be willing for five minutes or so to meet with a member of his constituency. It would be best if you pick a time when there is a bill that interests or concerns you that you could discuss with your elected representative.

After you have had a couple minutes to state your concerns and hear the response of your representative, you could ask your elected official to briefly explain the legislative process to your daughter. Such an explanation will be more succinct, more real, and more memorable to your daughter than any amount of "book learning."

5. Your daughter should understand the issues of the day.

To accomplish this level of understanding, your daughter should understand current events and more. Your daughter needs to know the events that are going on in society around her, plus a perspective on what is right and what is wrong. This perspective will come mainly from you. Fortunately this is a lot easier than it may sound.

You and your daughter will know more about current events than the world about you if you do three very simple things.

- *Read more news than you watch.* Having been the subject of many news stories, I can tell you that the print media is by far the more appropriate place to obtain accurate information about the news. Regular national TV news is built on the twenty-second sound-bite. It is superficial and tends to be the most biased. It is a good habit to get your daughter to read some news in the paper every day.

- *Read and discuss one news item at dinner.* If you would read an interesting news item and lead a short family discussion of it each night, the cumulative effect of this practice will be to raise children that are among the most "civic-literate" group in America. It will guarantee that your children understand your perspective on the news.

- *Read one Christian "hard news" publication.* Most Christian magazines are not news magazines but have some other kind of orientation. *World* magazine is a true weekly news magazine written from a solid Christian perspective. My older daughters read it regularly, as do I. *Citizen* magazine (published by *Focus on the Family*) is also excellent.

  Also Christian radio has two excellent news sources: "USA Radio," affiliated with Marlin Maddoux, and "Family News in Focus" are both highly professional sources to obtain news and a Christian perspective.

Four Things Your Daughter Should "Know How to Do" to be an Effective Citizen

1. Your daughter should know how to evaluate candidates for office.

There are three basic criteria to use to judge candidates: *character, issues,* and *qualifications.* If you will use these criteria yourself and discuss them with your daughter, she will learn a lot by watching you.

The best list of character qualifications I know of to use to evaluate political candidates is the standards for elders found in 1 Timothy 3:2. Ask yourself if the candidate is

above reproach
the husband of one wife (i.e., a faithful spouse)
temperate
self-controlled
respectable
hospitable (a sign of a servant's attitude)
able to teach
not given to drunkenness
gentle, not violent
not quarrelsome
not a lover of money
a good manager of his own family (obedient children)
not conceited
of good reputation.

I realize that this list would disqualify the vast majority of the members of Congress. Does it surprise you that our nation is in chaos? We elect people whose lives are a mess and we act surprised when they do the same thing to our nation.

We are involved in a group called "The Madison Project." Not only is it named after James Madison, the chief architect of the Constitution, but the letters M-A-D-I-S-O-N spell out "Make A Difference In Saving Our Nation." Its purpose is to help elect people who don't need to be lobbied. The long-range goal of the Madison Project is to elect pro-family, pro-life, economic conservatives who have steadfast values. Madison's goal is to find 1,000 members in every congressional district who will give $10 to five different candidates for Congress. This would raise over $20 million each election for our kind of candidates and would be the largest political fundraising organization in the nation. We are behind on votes in Washington because we don't get behind the right kind of candidates ahead of time.[3]

I know of no published source for character information on candidates. If you want to find out whether a candidate fits these biblical character qualifications, ask someone who knows them personally. For local offices you can usually find an appropriate source of information.

If not, watch the way they run their campaign. If a candidate does nothing but attack his or her opponent, you have a pretty good indication that the candidate fails the "not quarrelsome" test.

Let me warn you about something. Almost all candidates say that they hate negative campaigning. And I think most mean what they say. But the reality is that time and again candidates feel that they have to use negative campaigning because it has proven to be effective over and over again. Why? Because voters punish the person being attacked more than they punish the attacker. The only way to reverse this trend is for voters to deliberately say, "I will not vote for a person who runs an attack ad against his opponent." (An ad that merely states that a certain person voted a certain way is not an attack ad.)

Talk about attack ads with your daughter and help her to understand the character issues involved.

You can usually find out if a candidate has been divorced. I believe that it is a fair generalization that a candidate who has been divorced *after* going into public office has given you strong evidence that he loves politics more than he loves his own family. I would rate open infidelity while in office at least as harshly, if not more so.

After character, you will want to learn where the candidate stands on the issues. You can usually find a voters' guide for state legislative offices, statewide offices (governor, lieutenant governor, attorney general, etc.), Congress, Senate, and president from groups like Concerned Women for America, the various family groups associated with Focus on the Family, or the Christian Coalition.

These voter guides are very helpful in evaluating candidates on the issues.

If you cannot find answers to your questions, find out where a candidate is going to have a public meeting (call his office and ask) and take your daughter along. Prepare a list of questions together before going (three or four key questions), then go and ask your questions. If this is not available, call a candidate's office (or home for very localized positions) and ask them to send you information on the candidate's positions you request. If you cannot get an answer—they probably would have answered your questions negatively (or else are too disorganized, which means that they would probably operate a government office in a disorganized manner).

All of this may sound like a lot of time. But there are two reasons it is worth every minute you invest. First, if you are bringing your daughter along with you, the learning experience is second to none. Second, tell your daughter the reason that you are spending the time to investigate candidates is that these people want to take a whole lot of your money (in the form of taxes) while they are in office and you want to make sure that they are going to spend it in a manner you approve. (And maybe even that they will want less of your money than the other guy.)

2. Your daughter should know how to help a good candidate.

After you have checked out a candidate and you find that they are good in terms of both character and issues, there are three things you should do and teach your daughter to do.

Give the candidate some money. Even if it is just $10, every dollar helps and it shows your daughter the very practical fact that candidates need money. Urge your daughter to baby-sit or do some other odd job and to give a portion of her own money

($5 or $10) to a candidate. If she can hand it to him or her personally, so much the better. I can tell you from personal experience it is both a profound and humbling experience to have a child hand you a campaign contribution. You (the candidate) feel very responsible to see that the child's money is used wisely. You know that the child worked hard and that any amount is a great sacrifice for a child. And I can guarantee you that a child who has given $5 to a candidate will pay very close attention to the election returns and will take both a victory and a loss very personally.

Help the candidate get his or her message to other people. One way you can do this is by organizing a meeting in your home. You can arrange to have a candidate running for almost any office come to your home if you will guarantee him or her an attendance of forty or fifty people. (It is wonderful to have kids there in addition to the adults, but in fairness to the candidate tell them the number of *adults* expected.) A candidate for the state legislature will come at any point in the election cycle to see this number of people. Until the last two or three weeks of an election campaign, a candidate for governor or Congress will probably come to your house for a crowd of fifty. If you can produce a hundred people, you can get them almost right up to the very end of the election.

If you have an event like this at your house, of course, your daughter should be an integral part of the event. She should help decorate (signs can be obtained from the campaign office). She can help make the ever-present plates of goodies. She can help pass out literature and stickers when people arrive.

If you want to get involved in a way other than a gathering in your home, you can help the candidate stuff envelopes, make calls, or hand out literature door-to-door or at special events.

When I ran for office we had two Saturdays when we endeavored (and essentially succeeded) to pass out a million pieces of literature in a single day. I can tell you that there were thousands of girls and boys who helped their parents in this process. And the army of young people that was trained in the process was worth every effort of my running.

Remember to vote. Take your daughter to the polls with you if at all possible. In many places your child can come right into the voting booth with you. If she feels like this is partly her decision and effort, she will take ownership of the notion of active citizenship that will never be shaken.

3. Your daughter should know how to express her opinion in writing.

By the time your daughter is twelve or thirteen, I would encourage you to have her write "practice" letters to the editor once a month or so. It is a great way to supplement her formal academic training, and is a terrific method for teaching her the logic of argument.

A good letter to the editor is short, makes a single point, and is interesting. After a few practices, send a letter in. You will be surprised; it is very likely to get published (especially if you give your daughter's age).

4. Your daughter should know how to pray effectively for both candidates and elected officials.

I strongly urge you to model this practice for your daughter. Together pray over current events. Pray regularly before elections. When an issue you care about is going through Congress, pray every day for the bill.

Far more women than men pray about political matters. And I am convinced that these prayers are the mightiest weapons in our arsenal. Train your daughter to pray for our nation and she will help to move it profoundly.

At the beginning of the chapter I promised you that I would explain how normal dads with normal daughters can have a great impact on our nation. After reading this chapter, you may feel like a person who has just had a nuclear physicist explain how easy it would be to build your own nuclear power plant.

I am convinced that if you and your daughter would just do *one* or *two* of these ideas, America would be a much better nation.

Small steps can move a school system, turn a city or state, or change the course of a nation.

You are investing in your daughter's future by helping her invest in the world she will live in as an adult.

Notes

1. Peter Marshall and David Manuel, *The Light & the Glory* (Grand Rapids, Mich.: Fleming Revell Co., 1977).
2. *America's Godly Heritage*, Wallbuilders, Aledo, Texas.
3. "The Madison Project" address is PO Box 479, Hamilton, VA 22068. It publishes information on candidates' substantive political positions.

An Easy "To Do List"

Reading a book such as this can be a lot like going to a seminar. I usually come from attending a seminar with a "to do list" longer than my arm. It can be quite demoralizing. In fact, it can feel exactly like trying to take a drink out of a fire hydrant.

In this final chapter, I want to give you an easy "to do list." Let's start with three things *you don't have to do.*

First, you don't have to accomplish everything all at once.

One of my favorite passages in Scripture is Exodus 23:29–30. God is talking to the children of Israel as they are standing on the brink of the Promised Land. They have been told they are going to have to march. They are going to have to fight. They are going to have to build. They are going to have to find homes for their families. They are going to have to drive out numerous nations who were living in the land. It was quite a daunting "to do list."

Here's what God told them:

"But I will not drive them [the other nations] out in
a single year, because the land would become desolate
and the wild animals too numerous for you. Little by
little I will drive them out before you, until you have
increased enough to take possession of the land."

Our God is a gracious God. He doesn't expect us to conquer
every foe all at once. He gives us time. He expects us to take
the land—He will soundly correct us if we decide to lay down
our weapons and quit—but God has realistic expectations. He
expects us to take on big jobs little by little.

In the case at hand, the big job—our biggest "enemy"—is
our own weakness and failure. We have so much to work on—
so many areas that need improvement. I believe that the same
gracious God who expected the children of Israel to take the
Promised Land little by little expects you to make improve-
ments in your fathering on the same schedule. Steady progress, deliberate action, but the total victory doesn't come all
at once.

Second, you don't have to be responsible for the results.

There is an important division of labor between you and
God. You are your daughter's earthly father. God is the heavenly Father. Got it?

Your job description is to be faithful and obedient. God's
job description includes all responsibility for ultimate results.

You have to also remember that your daughter is a free
moral agent, and in many ways she will make her own decisions to do right or to do wrong.

There will be periods of her life when your daughter will
bring heartaches and turmoil. Despite all of the positive things
I've said about our daughters, let me assure you that when it
comes to turmoil—I've been there and done that. But so far,

the turmoil with our girls has been for a season that has in each case come to an end.

When you are in the midst of one of those seasons of trouble, if you have been faithful as a father you are going to feel a lot better than if you have been basically AWOL in your daughter's life.

If you have done your best—most of the time—then approach these seasons of turmoil with the confidence that comes from knowing that your heavenly Father loves your daughter far more than you. He will embrace her in His love even when the difficulties may be so pronounced that she will not accept even a hug from you.

God will bring her through, and give you the hope that He can bring her home to you.

Third, you don't have to do this alone.

Obviously, parenting is intended to be a two-person task with a father and a mother. You are well aware that more and more parents are facing the responsibility of going it alone.

But in addition to your wife, you can find strength and encouragement if you will find one or more men with whom you can share your father-daughter experience. Maybe it will be the father of one of your daughter's friends. You may want to go on outings together as a foursome.

But whether or not your daughter has a relationship with "his" daughter, you may find great encouragement from periodic fellowship with another man who is walking the same path.

That's my list of things you *don't* have to do. Let's consider two final things you should do.

Pray for your daughter every day.

If you remember nothing else from this book, remember to simply pray for your daughter every day. God, in His great mystery, has chosen to work among us in response to prayer.

Prayer is a gauge of your love for both God and your daughter. Prayer will keep your heart tender toward that precious life with whom you have been entrusted. Prayer will keep a channel open to God so He can more readily prompt you to remember to do what is right with your little girl. Prayer will help you remain aware of your responsibility to lead your daughter toward spiritual maturity.

You should pray for your daughter's development as a woman and eventually a wife and mother. You should pray for the young man He is preparing for her someday. You should pray for protection for your daughter as she moves through the wicked world that she will encounter at school, in sports, at work, and sometimes at church.

You should pray that she will learn to love and obey God's Word. And pray that she will readily share the love of God with those she calls her friends.

Pray that she will be a wise steward of her time and resources. And that she will work faithfully as a citizen of this land that has been so blessed by God.

And for a thousand other things, remember to pray for your daughter.

Do it now.

James Dobson once said, "Remember, we're not actually raising *children*, we're raising *adults*." We are training our daughters for the long haul. We want them to become responsible, mature women of God.

But the days of our influence are exceedingly fleeting. The day I wrote this chapter I talked to my daughter Christy on the phone from college. We talk several times a week. In some ways it seems that she has never gone. But in other ways I know my days of training with Christy are coming to a rapid conclusion. You have heard lots of people tell you the time goes very fast. Don't you believe them. It goes *a lot faster* than they have let on.

If you *don't* want to be suddenly surprised with a young woman you don't know and don't particularly care for because of her behavior and character, then, Dad, *begin now*.

If you want a daughter who handles money responsibly as an adult, rather than one who passes bad checks, teach her about money and responsibility *now*. If you want a daughter who is spiritually mature and is able to trust in God in all of life's circumstances and trials, you need to begin teaching her about God *now*. If you want a daughter who is emotionally and physically pure, unstained by the bizarre sexuality of our day, begin training her *now*.

If you want deep conversations when she is older, talk with her *now* while she's young. If you want to be able to guide her in her career, show yourself capable of guiding her through a third-grade math assignment *now*.

I like to play golf. (*Note*: I did not say that I am a golfer.) I am getting better, but I need a lot of practice. No one gets good at golf all at once. It takes instruction and practice and practice and practice. There are a lot of things to remember. And there are a lot of different skills to learn and, hopefully, begin to master. No one is a scratch-handicapper without a lot of work and a lot of review.

Anything of real value requires at least as much work as it takes to improve your golf game. Becoming a good father is no exception.

The vision you have for a lovely, mature daughter is, at least in part, a vision for yourself. It is a vision of the man you want to become. Being a dad takes a lot of hard work. You'll make mistakes. But you get a lot of chances to practice.

I have a glimpse of what it is like to finish the task of raising a young woman to maturity. I can see the finish line. And let me tell you that the experience of having a daughter who pleases both her earthly and heavenly Father is a greater thrill than a hole-in-one any day.

Begin now, because . . .

The Day Will Come When She Leaves Home

It was the moment I'd been preparing for. It was the moment I'd been dreading.

Christy was nineteen. She had delayed entering college for a year so she could work on my campaign as my Deputy Press Secretary. Now we were driving her to Ohio to leave her . . . 400 miles from home. Vickie and I—and our year-old son, Joey—drove in one car. Christy followed behind in her 1986 Ford Escort.

Waves of emotions and tears swept over both Vickie and me at several points that weekend. The worst was when we had to give her the final hug and say goodbye. Christy was calm and happy. After we drove away, her mother and I cried off-and-on for at least a hundred miles.

Sure, I'd expected to miss her. I realized how much I had come to depend on her to give me good advice in my ongoing dealings with the press. But at a deeper level, I knew that a strong part of my emotional reaction was a recognition that the season of her life when I could have daily fatherhood input was over.

Had I done enough? What would happen? How could I have done better? These kinds of questions swirled just below the surface of my emotions.

————

The intervening two years have done much to assuage my emotions. The sense of finality is not nearly as strong now as at the beginning of college. Breaks, plus lots of phone calls, still give us numerous opportunities for important interactions. But, it *is* different. The real comfort has come from seeing Christy do so well.

Not only is her GPA at 3.9+, not only has she been elected vice-president of her college's student body, far more importantly, we have seen Christy walking with God and walking among her fellowmen with the kind of spiritual and personal maturity that we had desired.

Try as you might to remember the doctrine of the sovereignty of God and the doctrine that your daughter has her own free will and is personally responsible to Him, you will judge yourself as a father based largely on your daughter's performance in adult life.

I have the evidence of two essentially grown daughters— Christy's story is easier to tell because Jayme has chosen to be apprenticed and stay at home for now. (Although she is leaving for a month in Romania in just a couple weeks.) And this evidence tells me that God is pretty gracious and compensates a great deal for my shortcomings. I have been far from the perfect father. I have learned most of what is written in this book while they have been growing up. I did not execute everything I know now during all those years.

But I can say with confidence that I gave Christy and Jayme a whole lot of time. And I can also say that I did many things right.

It is an awesome responsibility to be a father. Your labors are evaluated in the life of someone you love dearly.

When you face that day when your daughter leaves home, more than anything else you will want the confidence that comes from knowing you have invested well in her life. She has received training and correction and guidance and a whole lot of love from her dad.

The day she leaves home will not seem like her final examination. It will seem like yours. You understand the sense of utter despair of a college student who walks into a final examination having skipped class and never opened a book. You do not—I guarantee, *you do not*—want to have that same feeling when your daughter is ready to leave.

Be diligent. Work hard. Pray much. Do your very best. And

I believe that God will bless your work with a grown-up lady of whom you can be immensely proud.

For Thought and Discussion

1. What can I begin to do right now to improve my fathering?
2. What have I been neglecting or resisting to do for too long? *Do it now.*